you know you're in
washington when...

Some Other Books in the Series

You Know You're In Series

you know you're in
washington when...

101 Quintessential Places, People, Events, Customs, Lingo, and Eats of the Evergreen State

Sharon Wootton and Maggie Savage

INSIDERS' GUIDE ®

GUILFORD, CONNECTICUT

AN IMPRINT OF THE GLOBE PEQUOT PRESS

INSIDERS' GUIDE®

Copyright © 2007 Morris Book Publishing, LLC

All rights reserved. No part of this book may be reproduced or transmitted in any form by
any means, electronic or mechanical, including photocopying and recording, or by any information storage and retrieval system, except as may be expressly permitted by the 1976
Copyright Act or by the publisher. Requests for permission should be made in writing to The
Globe Pequot Press, P.O. Box 480, Guilford, Connecticut 06437.

Insiders' Guide is a registered trademark of Morris Book Publishing, LLC.

Text design by Linda R. Loiewski
Illustrations by Sue Mattero

Library of Congress Cataloging-in-Publication Data
Wootton, Sharon.
  You know you're in Washington when— : 101 quintessential places, people, events,
customs, lingo, and eats of the Evergreen State / Sharon Wootton and Maggie Savage.
— 1st ed.
    p. cm. — (You know you're in series)
  Includes index.
  ISBN-13: 978-0-7627-4301-8
  ISBN-10: 0-7627-4301-8
  1. Washington (State)—Miscellanea. 2. Washington (State)—Description and travel—
Miscellanea. I. Savage, Maggie. II.Title.
  F891.6.W66 2007
  979.7—dc22

                                                                    2006039747

Manufactured in the United States of America
First Edition/First Printing

To our dear friend Frank Varga

about the authors

Sharon Wootton, a Washington resident since 1974, has more than 3 million words in print as a journalist, columnist for two daily newspapers, and full-time freelance writer. Her stories have appeared in dozens of magazines and newspapers.

When **Maggie Savage,** a Washington native, isn't writing songs or performing them, she's wandering the Northwest and turning her experiences into travel stories.

Maggie and Sharon are co-owners of Song & Word (www.songandword.com), which offers writing and songwriting workshops and retreats for women in the San Juan Islands, where they live.

to the reader

Welcome to the sometimes quirky but often spectacular Evergreen State. Washington is blessed with crashing ocean waves and waves of grain, with mountains of both majesty and the potential for massive destruction.

Our landscape allows us to walk inside a lava flow, climb the peak of Mount Rainier, raft through whitewater rapids, puzzle over the origins of the mysterious Mima Mounds, and traverse channeled scablands.

Pacific storms dump enough rain to make western Washington permanently green, creating old-growth trees that are jaw-dropping marvels. Yet the Cascade Mountains block most of the rain from reaching the eastern two-thirds of the state, creating a landscape closer to the Midwest than the coast.

Washington is a state rich in entrepreneurship as well as natural wonders. Our best-known former teenage hackers, Bill Gates and Paul Allen, grew up to start Microsoft. Other Washington-based businesses that made it big include UPS, Nordstrom, Eddie Bauer, Starbucks, REI, Costco, and Amazon.

Washingtonians often have their noses in a book (check out the ferry passengers). We love reading so much, in fact, that one librarian has her own bobblehead doll. Yet we also embrace outdoor activities 365 days a year and root for college and professional sports teams.

Occasionally we're considered a bit otherworldly, and we're not talking about the Space Needle. The state is home to both the Science Fiction Museum and the National UFO Reporting Center—which makes sense given that the phrase "flying saucers" was coined in Washington when a pilot reported seeing nine unidentified objects flying near Mount Rainier.

Back on the ground Washingtonians are comfortable with having a female governor and two female U.S. senators—at the same time—without making a big deal of it. But this state, divided by a mountain range, is likewise split by politics. Color us purple: blue in the west, red in the east.

Residents are also comfortable with wearing hiking boots in downtown Seattle, and most care more about what's new in outdoor gear than the latest fashion trend. It all goes with our laid-back attitude. It's pretty hard to affect superiority when your best-loved characters are Ivar Haglund (King of Clams), Bobo the Gorilla, and Sasquatch.

Besides, we've had our share of humbling experiences: We have the three longest floating bridges in the world, but two of them have sunk. The largest nuclear-waste dump in the Western Hemisphere is in Washington (and it's leaking).

At least we can brag about the length of our banana slugs . . . and we do on page 2. Start your journey through quintessential Washington there, if you'd like, and enjoy the adventure.

you know you're in
washington when...
...you go inside the lava flow

It's not an adventure for the claustrophobic, but exploring Ape Cave offers a look into the heart of a lava flow.

About 2,000 years ago eruptions sent molten lava pouring down Mount St. Helens's southern slopes. While flowing down one of the creek beds, the top and sides of the lava cooled, forming a crust. Underneath, hot lava continued to flow away. What remained is the longest lava tube on the U.S. mainland and one of the longest continuous lava tubes in the world. The 12,810-foot tube is accessible to the public.

Since then three eruptions have sent mudflows oozing through Ape Cave, and volcanic sand has washed into the lower entrance. Each of these activities has left its mark. Inside the tube, sights include the 70-foot-wide Big Room with its 30-foot-high ceiling. In other sections 3-foot-deep fluted gutters line some walls, formed by the smaller lava streams that followed the main flow, causing the lava level to rise, start to congeal, and then leave the ledges as it receded.

In some places light shines through the ceiling; in others, the ceiling might be 30 feet thick. A few stalactites hang from above, created by dripping lava; stalagmites have built up from the floor from those drips.

Ape Cave:

This Mount St. Helens attraction is one of the world's longest continuous lava tubes.

Logger Lawrence Johnson accidentally discovered the entrance to Ape Cave sometime around 1950 (the exact date is disputed). The area went unexplored for a few years until a Boy Scout troop left footprints in the pristine dust. The tube was named in honor of the troop's sponsor, the St. Helen Apes, a group mostly of foresters.

More than 100,000 visitors a year explore Ape Cave, and during the summer, a naturalist leads tours through the lower part. Most of the walk ranges from crawl-space height to 7 feet. Light sources are needed (lanterns can be rented). The entrance to both sections of the tube is in the middle. The smoother route dead-ends in approximately three-quarters of a mile; the rougher walk is about a mile long.

North America's largest land mollusk, the banana slug, prowls moist forest floors in Washington State. Not a peewee like other slugs and snails, *Ariolimax columbianus* grows 8 to 10 inches long, a couple of inches shy of Europe's *Limax cinereoniger*.

The banana slug was nominated for the new Washington State quarter but didn't make the final cut. The Northwest's only large native slug is sometimes mistaken for the destructive slugs found in gardens and thus killed with zeal (and sometimes salt).

The slug is basically a soft body with a muscular foot and sandpaper-like grinding mouth parts that munch dead plant material, animal droppings, and some live plants as well. The eye stalks at the top of a slug's head detect light and movement. Another pair of sensory stalks can detect chemical smells.

Aptly named, the banana slug has a lemon-yellow body with black spots, although it can come in different colors (green, pale brown, and even black).

Sex and the single slug can be . . . an adventure. A ready-to-mate slug leaves a chemical come-on in its slime trail; another slug follows that chemical to the promised land. Each slug has male and female reproductive gear and produces eggs and sperm simultaneously. The mating dance can last 12 hours or more, much of it spent twisting

Banana Slug:

The second largest slug in the world has only its slime as protection against predators.

into eye-popping positions as the two slugs try to separate. Breaking up is hard to do because their penises are several inches long, and both are inserted. The slug who escapes first often does so by chewing off its partner's pride and joy.

Slugs evolved from snails, trading in protective shells for slime that allows them to glide slowly on waves of muscles (moving from back to front), reaching speeds of .007 miles per hour. Slime covers the slug's single foot, protects the soft body from sharp edges, and moistens the skin so that the slug can breathe. Slime also helps discourage predators. It becomes more goolike in the predator's mouth, where it reacts with moisture and releases a mild anesthetic.

Perhaps that's why you can find escargot in restaurants and not slugs.

you know you're in
washington when...
...bluebirds return to a dot on the map

The self-proclaimed Bluebird Capital of the World is a town of about 100 residents surrounded by wheat fields in south-central Washington, 20 miles north of the Columbia River. Bluebirds flock to Bickleton every spring, drawn by about 2,500 nesting boxes. The North American Bluebird Society honored the town in 1983.

Bickleton's other claims to fame are the state's oldest rodeo, a 1905 horse carousel that is kept in a secret vault and brought out during the annual Pioneer Picnic, one of the state's oldest taverns (the Bluebird Inn), and the Whoop-N-Holler Museum.

Thanks to Jess and Elva Brinkerhoff, Bickleton is on the radar of bluebirds and birdwatchers. The Brinkerhoffs were picnicking near Bickleton in the mid-1960s when they spotted a bluebird searching for a home, a tough assignment in the near-treeless wheat country. Operating on the theory that if you build it, they will come, Jess nailed a gallon can to a tree, and the bird moved in.

Eventually the Brinkerhoffs built as many as 2,000 bluebird houses and nailed them to trees and fenceposts in a 150-square-mile area around the town.

For the bluebirds, the blue-and-white homes replaced the nesting sites decimated by expanding farmlands that needed tillable land, not trees or snags with natural cavities for bluebird nests.

Around Valentine's Day the bright blue males (mostly mountain bluebirds) start to trickle in and vie for the best houses. Females arrive in March, and by late spring, everyone is in connubial bliss. Then the babies arrive, eventually learning to hover in insect-hunting mode before attacking their meals. In October everyone heads south.

During prime viewing season busloads of tourists arrive, looking for bluebirds. The town also boasts a blue-and-white birdhouse-shaped memorial to the Brinkerhoffs and a volunteer program to clean and paint the birdhouses, including one with a steeple outside a local church.

The area has gone to the birds, and the bluebirds love it.

Bluebird Capital:

Bickleton residents are outnumbered by the thousands when bluebirds return each spring.

We gave our hearts to Bobo. One family named their son after him; Bobo even received write-in votes for mayor.

Bobo, a baby gorilla, was taken from Africa in 1951 by "Gorilla Bill" Said and left with Said's mother in Ohio. Anacortes fisherman Bill Lowman bought the primate for $4,000; caretaking responsibility fell to *his* mother, Jean. (Where would we be without our mothers . . . ?)

Bobo reached stardom through articles and television. Lowman's daughters played with Bobo; he went to the drive-in, enjoyed music, and ate at the dinner table.

But Bobo taught us a lesson: It's impossible to change evolution and turn a gorilla into a child. By age 22 months Bobo had grown into a primate wrecking ball and was tearfully sold to Seattle's Woodland Park Zoo for $5,500. Jean Lowman stayed with him for weeks before her family literally had to tear her away, Bobo holding on to her leg.

He lived in the Great Ape House for 15 years, a 6.5-foot, 520-pound attraction. Bobo destroyed his birthday cake to peals of children's laughter, grumpily charged the viewing window, and steadfastly refused to mate with fellow captive Fifi.

Bobo died in 1968 of a fracture of the larynx with hemorrhaging that resulted in asphyxia. His obituary made the front page of the *Seattle Post-Intelligencer*.

Taxidermists stuffed Bobo for display at the Museum of History and Industry in Seattle. Somewhere along the line his skull mysteriously disappeared. Eventually Bobo was put into storage and neglected. In 2000 taxidermists gave him a makeover, fluffing, vacuuming, and rehabbing his pelt. Today, the museum throws an annual bash for Bobo.

Another Washington gorilla was Ivan, who spent 27 years in solitary confinement in a Tacoma shopping mall after being sold to the owner of the B & I department store in 1964. The Progressive Animal Welfare Society waged a seven-year campaign to free the silverback gorilla, who eventually was given to Woodland Park Zoo and then permanently loaned to Zoo Atlanta in 1995.

Bobo:

This gorilla, a star attraction at Woodland Park Zoo, touched many Washingtonians' hearts.

4

Although the Boeing Company's public image is linked to commercial airplanes, it owes much to its military connections.

William Boeing, son of a wealthy Detroit family, arrived in Washington in 1903 to invest in the timber industry. He soon fell in love with the newfangled flying machines. In 1915 Boeing and engineer George Westervelt began building a twin-float seaplane in a boathouse, the seed for the Boeing Airplane Company.

The Navy ordered dozens of planes for World War I, the beginning of Boeing's boom-and-bust cycles. The company struggled postwar, building furniture and flat-bottomed boats, but rebounded with a 1921 Army order for more than 200 fighter biplanes.

When Boeing won a federal airmail contract in 1927 (for the San Francisco to Chicago route), it added seats for two passengers on each biplane flight. That first year Boeing moved 1,863 passengers and glimpsed the future. It built the first plane designed to carry passengers, a 12-seat biplane with hot and cold running water, a toilet, and registered nurses as stewardesses.

But Boeing soon was accused of monopolistic practices and split into three companies, including the Boeing Airplane Company and United Air Lines. In 1934 William Boeing retired to become a thoroughbred horse breeder.

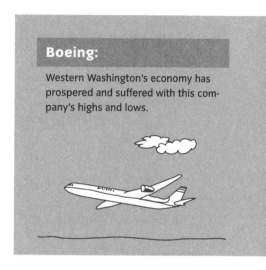

Boeing:

Western Washington's economy has prospered and suffered with this company's highs and lows.

In World War II Boeing rolled out B-17s and B-29s; postwar, Seattle's largest employer cut 70,000 jobs. In 1954 the prototype of the Boeing 707, a jetliner not a propeller-driven plane, cut coast-to-coast travel time in half, drove down fares, and changed the face of commercial aviation.

Another boom and bust followed from 1969 to 1971, when the Boeing payroll fell from 109,000 to about 38,000 employees. The area's economy suffered so badly that a billboard sign asked, "Would the last person who leaves Seattle please turn out the lights?" Yet Boeing persevered to become the world's leading producer of commercial passenger and military aircraft (combined).

About 65,500 of Boeing's 154,000 employees are in Washington State.

Where could you put 911 National Basketball Association courts under one roof? Or 2,142 homes, each about 2,000 square feet?

They would fit in the world's largest building (by volume) in the world: the Boeing Company's 472-million-cubic-foot jet-assembly plant, which covers 98 acres in Everett.

The six doors to the plant are equally impressive, each 82 feet high by 300 to 350 feet wide. On them is the world's largest digital graphic, comprising more than 100,000 square feet of pressure-sensitive graphic film. (The graphic took five months to install, partly because someone decided it was a good thing to start during Washington's rainy season.)

The far left door shows a young woman with her head thrown back, eyes closed, feeling the sunshine on a blue-sky day. The next five doors are shots of blue skies and Boeing airplane sections.

When Boeing decided in 1966 to build what was then the world's largest airplane, it had to construct a building to match the goal. What started out at 200 million cubic feet increased as airplanes got larger. Today, plane components arrive from around the world by ship, truck, rail, and air. Parts from

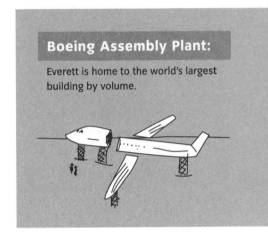

Boeing Assembly Plant:

Everett is home to the world's largest building by volume.

ships are loaded on rail cars that can be rolled inside the assembly building.

Boeing's weekday tours of the assembly plant draw more than 110,000 people a year from around the world. They're usually awed by the sheer size of the interior, huge overhead bridge cranes (which operate 90 feet above the floor), thousands of people working on planes, and more than 100 forklifts delivering parts.

Visitors can also explore exhibits at the nearby Future of Flight Aviation Center and Boeing Tour. There they can ride a multipassenger XJ5 flight simulator, digitally design and test a jet, and touch the high-tech skin of the 787 Dreamliner.

washington when...

...fish tales reach the U.S. Supreme Court

The state's biggest fish tale includes prejudice, protest, gunfire, treaties, an 1818 dictionary, and a stunning power shift.

In 1854–1855 six treaties, designed to take most of the Native Americans' western Washington land, were signed. One clause, or a variation of it, in all six treaties protected Indians' traditional right to fish. That clause was quickly ignored by non-Indians, who over the next century increased in number, overfished salmon with commercial boats, destroyed habitats, built dams, polluted the water, and blamed the Indians for declining fish runs because the tribes didn't obey the state's fishing rules. Tribe members, who often fished at night to avoid run-ins with fishery officials, caught only about 5 percent of the salmon. Yet the Fish Wars of the 1960s were bitter. The state wanted to tell the tribes when, where, and how they could fish; for the tribes, salmon fishing was a treaty right, their main source of revenue, and part of their culture. Raids, surveillance planes, arrests, guns, beatings, and tear gas were used to fight the "poachers." The tribes countered with fish-ins and national media attention, courtesy of support from Jane Fonda, Marlon Brando, and Nisqually activist Billy Frank, deemed a "renegade" for his leadership and arrests for protest fishing.

Finally the federal government, citing the treaties, sued the state. Conservative U.S. District Court Judge George Boldt, an avid sports fisherman, presided. In 1974 Boldt shocked everyone. Using an 1818 *Webster's American Dictionary* to help him interpret "in common with," Boldt ruled that the tribes were entitled to up to 50 percent of the harvestable salmon and steelhead in their traditional fishing grounds. The Boldt Decision, one of the most significant rulings in Indian law, also made the tribes comanagers of the fisheries with the state, an unheard-of sharing of power. It enraged non-Indians, but the U.S. Supreme Court upheld the 50–50 allocation and Boldt's general principles. The decision was a factor in reducing the size of the nontribal commercial fishing fleet, reducing recreational fishers' salmon share, and creating a bitterness that lingers today.

Boldt Decision:

This 1974 ruling upheld Native American rights to up to 50 percent of the salmon caught in traditional fishing grounds.

you know you're in
washington when...
...the librarian has her own bobblehead doll

Sure, Mariners all-star outfielder Ichiro Suzuki is immortalized in a bobblehead figure, but so is Nancy Pearl, the Seattle librarian turned action figure. Her bobblehead has push-button "shushing" and comes with bookmarks.

Pearl is author of the best-selling *Book Lust* and its successful follow-up, *More Book Lust.* As the former executive director of the Washington Center for the Book at the Seattle Public Library, she started the "If All Seattle Read the Same Book" program, which many other cities have adopted.

Pearl has become the reader's rock star, with a monthly television program on a public-access channel and commentary on National Public Radio's *Morning Edition* and two NPR affiliates. An all-star librarian might surprise the rest of the nation but not Seattle, the most literate city in the country, according to a 2005 survey, as well as the leader in using Internet resources.

The Seattle Public Library may have the largest percentage of active library-card holders per capita in the nation (80 percent), and its residents spend twice the national annual average on books, leading to a number-one ranking in the ratio of booksellers to population. Seattle also has the nation's highest percentage of residents with a college degree.

Bookworms:

Seattle is the most literate city in the nation.

In Seattle books are in backpacks, briefcases, and bookbags. The rest of Washington reads, too, particularly when commuting by ferry to Seattle.

Authors who have ties to greater Seattle include Tom Robbins, Rebecca Brown, David Guterson, Sherman Alexie, Terry Brooks, John Saul, J. A. Jance, Greg Bear, Ann Rule, Vonda McIntyre, Jack Olsen, John Vance, and Elizabeth Julesburg (who created the first *Dick and Jane* children's book series under the pseudonym Elizabeth Montgomery).

Scientists wear hard hats when studying treetops from the world's largest canopy crane 10 miles from the Columbia River Gorge.

The Wind River crane, similar to machinery used in urban areas, carries researchers aloft in a gondola, providing access to more than 300 trees across six acres. The gondola can clear 220-foot-tall trees, return to the same branch on a specific tree when needed, and cover a circle 550 feet across.

Four days and two other cranes were needed to install the $620,000, 190-ton crane, erected in 1995. Of the world's 10 operating canopy cranes, the Wind River machine has the most extensive research program, can access the largest area of forest, and is the second tallest. It was the first erected in a temperate forest. The Wind River Canopy Crane Research Facility is a joint effort of the University of Washington, the U.S. Forest Service, and the Gifford Pinchot National Forest.

The crane operator climbs 300 rungs on a series of ladders, a trip that takes at least seven minutes. Researchers pay $182 an hour to use the machine.

Treetops and branch tips interest scientists because that's where most of photosynthesis, budding, and branching occur. It's the best place to study how trees absorb the greenhouse gas carbon dioxide, how forest evaporation might cool the earth, how trees are affected by pollution, and how old-growth forest differs from young forests.

Research has yielded some interesting results. It once was assumed, for example, that because young trees grow faster, young forests absorb far more carbon dioxide than old-growth forests. But researchers have learned that old-growth forests store huge amounts of carbon dioxide.

Another assumption was that trees go dormant in the winter. Research shows that they don't. Photosynthesis slows down, but because of lack of sunlight, not because of cold.

Sorry, the public can't enter the Wind River facility because of safety concerns and the need for a pristine research area.

Canopy Crane:

The 25-story Wind River canopy crane helps scientists study the treetops in western Washington.

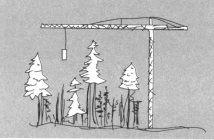

A geological sacred cow died on the Columbia Plateau, where the channeled scablands cover 75 percent of eastern Washington. Until the 1920s geologists believed that this nearly barren, deeply carved landscape was created by retreating glaciers and erosion. But geologist J. Harlan Bretz could not make the channeled scablands, a term he coined, fit the model. He proposed the geological equivalent of "The emperor has no clothes." Bretz said that catastrophic flooding of the high-desert plateau, the world's second largest lava field, created the scablands. His words ignited a hot geology battle.

Bretz's theory was that at the end of the last Ice Age, a 3,000-square-mile lake up to 2,000 feet deep had been formed by an ice dam in western Montana. When the dam broke, the water of Glacier Lake Missoula raced across the Idaho panhandle and onto Washington's southward-sloping plateau, with water hundreds of feet deep rushing at up to 65 miles per hour.

This deluge sculpted the landscape into coulees (steep ravines), canyons, buttes, and boulder fields, scrubbing bare about 2,000 square miles right down to the basalt. One of the largest gouged-out channels was Grand Coulee Canyon, 50 miles long and 1 to 5 miles across.

The longer he looked, the more evidence Bretz gathered of moving water creating geologic formations in the now-arid countryside. Bretz found plunge pools, undercutting, and cataract retreat—indicating waterfalls, not a retreating glacier.

The two largest waterfalls were the Upper Coulee, where a river once roared over an 800-foot cliff, and Dry Falls near Soap Lake. In both cases the waterfalls had eroded miles upstream as basalt sections were washed away.

By 1965, after more geologists studied the area and aerial photography helped show the patterns, Bretz's theory was accepted. Geologists now call the event the Missoula Flood, the Bretz Flood, the Spokane Flood, or the Ice Age Flood, although there's disagreement over whether it was one huge flood or several catastrophic floods.

Channeled Scablands:

A cataclysmic flood at the end of the Ice Age etched much of eastern Washington into this signature landscape.

Among its other achievements, the Seattle area is second only to Venice in the number of glassblowing studios and skilled glassblowers.

Thank Tacoma-born Dale Chihuly, who put Washington State on the glassblowing map.

Chihuly revolutionized the Studio Glass movement (whose members believed they were creating art, not just a product) by emphasizing collaborative glassblowing teams in the Pilchuck Glass School, which he cofounded in Stanwood.

The first person to be named a U.S. Living National Treasure, Chihuly was also the first American glassblower to work at the renowned Venini Fabrica in Italy. He has pushed the glass world's boundaries, creating large, often lopsided contemporary glass sculptures (rather than traditional small, centered pieces) and building multipart compositions and room-size installations. He lives and works in a huge boathouse on Lake Union.

An auto accident cost Chihuly an eye in 1976, giving him his signature eyepatch. His lack of depth perception and a shoulder injury stopped him from handling molten glass. Now he creates the concepts, and a team of glassblowers carries them out.

Chihuly escapes the artificial boundaries of art and craft and sets out in a parallel universe where his vision rules. There's an element of playfulness to his sculptures: They captivate, writhe, stun, and flow. His passion for abstract flower forms and love of the sea often reflect the Northwest.

Chihuly usually thinks big, from the $12 million Chihuly Bridge of Glass in Tacoma to a Kew Gardens exhibit in London. More than 200 museums have Chihuly pieces, including the artist-inspired Museum of Glass in Tacoma.

But Chihuly also has become embroiled in lawsuits, claiming copyright infringement by other glassblowers—cases that could have ramifications about artistic expression.

Chihuly, Dale:

This Tacoma native revolutionized the Studio Glass movement with his creative vision and support for glassblowing teams.

you know you're in
washington when...
...dragons and dim sum share the streets

Seattle's Chinatown/International District is about 50 blocks of sensory experience and immigration history—and the scene of one of Seattle's biggest crimes.

Old and new fit together here, with traditional celebrations of the Chinese New Year (complete with dragons), healing arts that reflect both modern and ancient practices, and restaurants that cover the culinary range of Asian foods. Walking in Chinatown is a delight to the senses: You'll encounter the aromas of incense, herbs, and roast duck; the sight of traditional Asian color combinations; and the sounds of many languages.

A visit is not complete without a stop at Uwajimaya, the largest Asian grocery and gift store in the Northwest.

In the 1860s Chinese immigrants were the first Asians to arrive in Seattle, providing labor for the fishing, lumber, and railroad industries. They established one of the oldest districts in Seattle, one that now is a cultural hub for Chinese, Japanese, Korean, Filipino, Vietnamese, and Laotian residents.

The Chinese were also the first Asians to be discriminated against once the railroads were completed. The Chinese Exclusion Act of 1882 prevented more Chinese laborers from arriving in the United States. Locals drove many Chinese residents from their homes and literally shipped some out of

Chinatown/International District:

The cultural hub for Seattle's Asian Americans dates back to the mid-1800s.

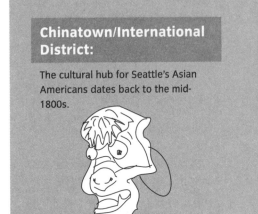

town. The Great Seattle Fire of 1899 burned down much of what was left of the community.

When the Jackson Street Regrade was finished in 1910, new buildings went up, and Chinatown was reborn. Eventually Chinatown became the International District. It was billed as an honor but really was a thinly veiled political attempt to contain those of African and Asian descent. Today, the area is officially known as the Seattle Chinatown Historic District.

The district is also the site of the 1983 Wah Mee Massacre. Three men robbed and shot 14 people in the Wah Mee high-stakes gambling club and stole tens of thousands of dollars. Thirteen died in the city's worst mass murder.

Imagine kayaks, tugboats, cabin cruisers, sailboats, and fishing boats floating cheek-by-jowl in a narrow concrete rectangle, waiting for the water level to rise (or fall) 6 to 26 feet before being flushed out into the next leg of their journey.

That is the scene at Seattle's Hiram C. Chittenden Locks, part of the 8-mile-long Lake Washington Ship Canal. The canal, which connects freshwater Lake Washington and Lake Union with saltwater Puget Sound, serves about 60,000 customers a year. When it opened, it was the second-largest canal in the Western Hemisphere, behind the Panama Canal.

Nearly since the founding of the city, plans had been floated to link the bodies of water. The aim was to compensate for the 35-foot differential between low tide on the Sound and on Lake Washington. Lake Union, located between these two waterways, was named after that concept.

Mill owners on Lake Union and Lake Washington pushed hard for "the ditch," and in 1908 U.S. Army Corps of Engineers Major Hiram Chittenden's proposal for concrete locks was approved. A boat parade dedicated the locks on July 4, 1917.

Now crowds line the walkways to watch watercraft that ordinarily wouldn't associate with each other—working boats and

million-dollar yachts, for example—share the ride. A 1,200-foot promenade includes a fishing pier, footbridge, and observation deck. Also in the area are the five-acre Carl S. English Jr. Botanical Garden, which features native plants and lawns for picnicking, and a visitor center that offers historical exhibits and explains lock operation.

On the south side of the complex, windows give a fish-eye view of sockeye, Chinook, coho, and steelhead climbing the 21-step fish ladder June through October. A viewing room at the 18th step allows visitors to watch the fish struggle against the current on their way to spawning grounds.

Chittenden Locks:

About 60,000 watercraft a year use these locks to pass between two freshwater lakes and saltwater Puget Sound.

13

It can be argued that Seattle has more—or fewer—than seven serious hills. But around the turn of the 20th century, people didn't quibble about whether a hill was really a ridge. They liked the lucky number and the link to Rome and thus gave Seattle an unlikely nickname: the City of Seven Hills.

It was an ironic marketing tool for a city that, about the same time, scraped off the top of one rise (Denny Hill), dumping it into Puget Sound to create the current waterfront and an industrial island. Other elevation-lowering efforts sent dirt into the tidelands on which the Mariners and Seahawks now play. Historians believe that city boosters counted the following hills among the seven:

Denny Hill: The once-steep hill was flattened in the early 1900s.

First Hill: King County's first courthouse was built on this rise, requiring downtown lawyers to climb the steep hill and leading to the nickname Profanity Hill. Today it's also known as Pill Hill because of the three major medical centers located there.

Second Hill: It was once called Renton Hill, after the man who owned and logged the ridge.

Yesler Hill: This formation could be considered the southernmost part of First Hill, but that gets in the way of the Magic Seven. It was named after a pioneer mill owner.

Capitol Hill: A developer promoting luxury homes near Volunteer Park named this hill in 1901 during a failed attempt to lure the state capital from Olympia. He offered 100 acres to build a new capitol.

Queen Anne Hill: Originally called Temperance Hill thanks to its numerous teetotalers, it's now known for mansions of the Queen Anne–architectural style.

Beacon Hill: More of a ridge than a hill, it was settled in 1851 but not formally named until 1899 by, you guessed it, a developer.

Some would argue for other candidates for the promotional seven, including West Seattle Hill, the highest point (520 feet) in Seattle. But Seattle wasn't laid out until after the City of Seven Hills slogan was created.

City of Seven Hills:

Seattle's steep hills are a challenge to climb but provide vistas of postcard proportions.

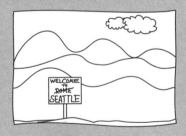

you know you're in
washington when...
... coffee shops are as common as raindrops

Washington has more coffee bean roasters per capita than any other state, and Seattle is the U.S. espresso capital, with more coffee shops per capita than any other city.

Thank coffee giant Starbucks, which might have been called Starbo, after a former mining camp on Mt. Rainier, or named Pequod, after Captain Ahab's ship in *Moby-Dick*. Both of those ideas were nixed in favor of Ahab's first mate, Starbuck—not surprising given the founding partners.

English teacher Jerry Baldwin, history teacher Zev Siegel, and writer Gordon Bowker opened Starbucks in 1971 in Seattle's Pike Place Market. They owed part of their inspiration to Holland immigrant and coffee seller Alfred Peet of Berkeley, California, who preached to them about quality bean-roasting techniques.

The trio initially concentrated on selling beans and brewing equipment. In 1982 they hired Howard Schultz as director of marketing, a move that would later transform Starbucks and make Schultz a billionaire.

On a trip to Milan, Italy, Schultz fell in love with the city's coffeehouses, each an experience with a friendly barista and camaraderie. The three partners wouldn't follow his vision, even when a test-market Italian–style espresso bar in the corner of a new Starbucks was an unqualified success.

Coffee Wars:

Starbucks and Seattle's Best Coffee battled for years until Starbucks bought its rival.

Schultz left the company in 1985 and opened his own espresso bar, Il Giornale, using Starbucks beans. Two years later Schultz bought Starbucks and implemented his saturate-a-market strategy.

Stewart Brothers Coffee, which had beat Starbucks to the Pike Place Market by a few months, was stiff competition. For years the two companies fought with distinctive blends in a war for taste buds and brand loyalty. The Stewart brothers later changed their company's name to SBC Inc., which led to the trade name Seattle's Best Coffee. It became the world's leading seller of specialty beans.

In 2003 Starbucks bought Seattle's Best Coffee. Today Starbucks has its own roasting plants, more than 7,100 company-owned stores in the United States and 37 countries, and more than 4,500 licensed or joint-venture outlets worldwide.

you know you're in
washington when...
...a river inspires dam builders and windsurfers

Inspiration for songwriters, environmentalists, and windsurfers alike, the Columbia River flows south out of British Columbia, entering Washington in the northeast corner of the state. Hundreds of miles later, it creates a 300-mile stretch of the Washington–Oregon border on its way to the Pacific Ocean.

It's the largest river by volume that flows into the Pacific from North America and the largest river in the world without a delta.

When fur trader and explorer Captain Robert Gray sailed along Washington's Pacific coast in 1792, he became the first white man to see the river. He named it after his ship, the *Columbia*.

The Columbia once was one of the top salmon-producing river systems in the world, but overfishing and a series of 11 dams and eight locks damaged that resource. On the plus side, nearly half of U.S. hydroelectricity comes from the Columbia river system, which provides water for more than a half-million otherwise arid acres of agriculture land. The Grand Coulee Dam and the Chief Joseph Dam are the top U.S. producers of hydroelectricity.

The Columbia inspired Woody Guthrie's "Roll On, Columbia" and "The Great Grand Coulee Dam," although a $270 paycheck from the government helped. In 1941 Guthrie was a Dust Bowl refugee hired to

Columbia River:

This behemoth flows 1,232 miles, starting from a British Columbia lake and proceeding south through Washington, then to the Pacific Ocean.

promote dam-building's benefits (namely, cheap electricity) by writing songs.

He wrote 26 songs in a month, including "Roll On, Columbia," aimed at encouraging rural residents to electrify their homes. It became Washington's official folk song.

The river also inspires environmentalists who work to protect much of the shoreline and to make the federal government keep its promise to clean up the Hanford Nuclear Reservation (see page 38), from which radioactive materials have leaked into the Columbia River.

The most spectacular stretch of the river is through the 80-mile-long Columbia Gorge. Winds 15 to 35 miles per hour blow through, making that stretch a mecca for windsurfers, kiteboarders, and sailboarders from around the world.

With $200,000 strapped to his body, a man named D. B. Cooper jumped from an airplane on November 24, 1971, parachuting from 10,000 feet over southwest Washington and into history. His act remains the world's only unsolved skyjacking.

Since then his story has been told in movies (*The Pursuit of D. B. Cooper* and *The Search for D. B. Cooper*); songs ("D. B. Cooper," "Bawitdaba," and "Bag Full of Money"); books, including a few by ex-FBI agents; an edition of the comic strip *The Far Side;* and the television show *Unsolved Mysteries.*

Cooper boarded the plane in Portland. Allegedly armed with a bomb, he forced the pilots to land in Seattle, where he exchanged hostages for his demands: $200,000 in cash and several parachutes. The plane took off and headed south. Cooper jumped and may have landed near Ariel.

Despite one of the most intensive manhunts in FBI history, Cooper was not found. In 1980, about $5,800 of the loot was discovered by a boy playing along the Columbia River near Vancouver. Out of more than 1,000 suspects, the most credible may have been Floridian Duane Weber, who on his deathbed in 1995 whispered to his wife that he was Cooper. His background lent credibility to this claim: He had a criminal record. He told his wife that he had injured his knee jumping out of a plane. He handwrote notes in a book on D. B. Cooper. He

generally matched Cooper's description. And he took a sentimental vacation along the Columbia.

Today, Cooper would be called a terrorist. Then, he was more like the little guy ripping off a large corporation, thumbing his nose at the FBI, and getting away with the perfect crime. Ironically, his crime helped create support for passenger screening. It also prompted the Federal Aviation Administration to fit all Boeing 727 planes with a mechanical wedge, dubbed a Cooper Vane, to prevent the rear stairway from opening during flight.

D. B. Cooper's legend continues. Ariel Store & Tavern in Ariel sponsors D. B. Cooper Days; a few stolen bills were auctioned on eBay in 2005; and in one episode of the Fox television series *Prison Break,* an inmate confesses to being D. B. Cooper.

Cooper, D. B.:

After extorting $200,000 he skyjacked an airliner and jumped out in 1971, never to be captured.

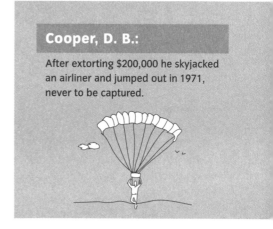

you know you're in
washington when...
...cougars wander into your backyard

In western Washington the "Not in My Backyard" (NIMBY) syndrome applies not only to toxic dumps and prisons but also to cougars.

People, in love with open space and wildlife, move to the country. Cougars are squeezed between suburbia and the mountains, resulting in increasing interactions between humans and animals. This makes humans uncomfortable, and they complain when cougars are in their backyards or confront them on hiking trails.

According to state Department of Fish and Wildlife biologists, the cougar population numbers about 3,000. Attacks on people are rare, although encounters are increasing. More attacks have occurred in the last two decades in western Canada and the United States than in the previous eight decades.

Also increasing are NIMBY complaints to the state Department of Fish and Wildlife, often resulting in the animals being relocated or, more often, killed (or, as the DFW puts it, "lethally removed").

Cougars have killed only a few people in the last 150 years. For a bit of perspective: More people die from drowning, bee stings, dog attacks, or lightning than from cougar attacks in Washington State.

Cougars are normally reclusive, but they do need to eat and might perceive a human as prey. Cougars may go after cats, dogs, and livestock. Deer are a dietary mainstay. Cougars are most active at dusk and dawn but will roam at any time of the day or night.

Their scientific name, *Felis concolor,* means "cat of one color"—in this case, uniformly gray to reddish tan. Adult male cougars can weigh more than 150 pounds and have a 3-foot-long tail.

If you encounter a cougar, also called a mountain lion, here are a few things to remember: Don't run (and pick up small children so they don't run). Stand tall or get up on a log or stump and wave your arms; shout and throw rocks or sticks. If a cougar attacks, fight back and remain standing.

Cougars:

About 3,000 cougars roam Washington's wild lands—and sometimes our backyards.

The extremely steep slope of Queen Anne Hill in Seattle made it one of the last areas to be developed. It was miserable for horses pulling wagons up the 18-percent grade, and walking up sucked the energy out of even the most able-bodied.

In 1902 a Seattle Electric Company streetcar line went up Queen Anne Avenue. The key to its success was hidden in a tunnel underneath the tracks. A narrow-gauge, waist-high railroad car with 16 tons of concrete, called a shoe, ran on a set of underground tracks. A hook-up man used a cable to attach it to the streetcar. The streetcar driver would start his vehicle, and the counterbalance would move in the opposite direction, assisting in the climb or preventing a runaway car on the descent.

This section of the route became known as The Counterbalance, and it's still called that today.

If the cable broke, the streetcar usually could stop, but the counterbalance would be out of control. Planners put sandbags at the bottom of the hill to cushion the impact of the sliding weight.

The streetcar's descent was not without excitement. The steep hill leveled off briefly, and the sudden change of direction jolted the streetcar and its passengers. It was not unusual for the conductor to shout, "Hang on!"

The Counterbalance:

Seattle's Queen Anne Hill is so steep that streetcars had to use a counterweight system to navigate it.

In 1937 there were plans for a new type of public transportation. A demonstration race pitted a streetcar and a trackless trolley on The Counterbalance. According to a *Seattle Times* article, the modern coach "embarrassed the Queen Anne streetcar," making it to the top of the 2,150-foot hill in less than half the time.

But voters, perhaps still shell-shocked from the Depression, rejected a plan to install the new system. The streetcar line limped along until 1940, when buses and trackless trolleys took over and the last counterbalance-assisted electric streetcar climbed Queen Anne Hill.

Today, a community group is exploring the possibility of an underground counterbalance tour, still possible because the old tunnel was never filled in.

Call them Rocky Mountain oysters if you want, but the stars of the Cowboy Caviar Fete in the north-central town of Conconully are still bull testicles.

Inspiration for the festival came out of folks just sitting around and talking. The conversation turned to castrating bull calves, the cut that turns a bull into a steer. The ranchers said castration wasn't a big thing anymore because rubber bands are used to keep the testicles from growing, which led to words about testicle festivals. Someone suggested starting one in Conconully as a companion to the Outhouse Races.

The organizers decided to go upscale with the inaugural Conconully testicle festival in 2003. Rather than take the deep-fry-and-serve approach, they started a culinary contest and called it the Cowboy Caviar Fete.

"It was a way to show off the quality of the three restaurants we have in town. They don't just serve tacos and hamburgers," says chamber of commerce spokeswoman Marilyn Church.

Because of the aforementioned rubber bands, the chamber had to order testicles from a restaurant supplier six months in advance. Once the cowboy caviar arrived, local chefs turned their creativity loose, producing Rocky Mountain oysters on the half shell, skewered bull balls, and testicles with pineapple and a little cocktail dressing.

Cowboy Caviar:

Conconully's Cowboy Caviar Fete features restaurants vying to create the best dish made with bull testicles.

The delicacies were soaked in various sauces, served whole or sliced.

"Spiced is always a big hit. They call it the Balls of Fire," Church says.

Visitors vote on the winner of the Balls to the Wall plaque.

Church swears that some brave souls travel the testicle-festival circuit: "People who really know say smaller balls are tastier than the bigger ones, but you have to cut the membrane off them, and the restaurants complain every minute. In 2005 we had a lot of mature bull balls, about the size of a tennis ball."

But how do they taste, Marilyn? "I've never eaten one. I'm not that adventurous."

Washington's relatively young chain of active, dormant, and dead volcanoes dominates the Cascade Range, splitting the state like a picket fence. These volcanoes, part of the Pacific Ring of Fire, have produced many of the known eruptions on the mainland United States. Long before white explorers "discovered" the volcanoes, Native Americans developed legends about mountains that exploded. One, named Tahoma by Lushootseed-speaking tribes, became Mount Rainier.

Rainier is king among the five largest volcanoes that dominate their shorter relatives, but Mount St. Helens often steals the show with periodic huffs and puffs and an expanding lava dome. Add Mount Adams, Mount Baker, and Glacier Peak, and you have a string of volcanoes that have erupted, in geologic terms, recently.

Cascade Range volcanoes have blown more than 200 times in 12,000 years, and some are considered dead. Volcanoes that have erupted in the last few centuries are considered active, but some volcanoes can be quiet (or dormant) for many centuries, even thousands of years, before exploding again.

Mount Baker exploded in 1880 for the first time in several thousand years and still has active steam vents. Mount Rainier, the tallest volcano in the United States outside of Alaska, has had four eruptions in the last

4,000 years, the last major eruption about 2,500 years ago.

Mount Adams had a series of small eruptions about 1,000 years ago. Glacier Peak has erupted at least six times in the last 4,000 years; a powerful series of eruptions about 13,000 years ago deposited ash at least as far away as Wyoming.

The most recent Cascade eruption was in 1980, when Mount St. Helens blew its top, literally disintegrating its picture-perfect snow-covered peak. Because volcanoes tend to repeat their behaviors and Mount St. Helens is the most frequently active volcano in the Cascades, it's likely that a similar eruption will happen . . . someday.

Dormant Volcanoes:

Several Washington volcanoes are quiet for now but could explode in the near future, geologically speaking.

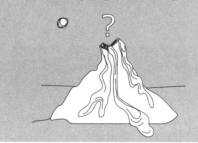

If you're from the East Coast and are fond of blue crabs, the phrase "genetic mutant" might spring to mind when you see a Dungeness crab. The average *Cancer magister* is just under 7 inches from shell tip to shell tip but can reach 8 to 10 inches. Blue crabs, on the other hand, average about 5 inches.

Dungeness crabs are prized for their texture, sweetness, and buttery flavor. They were first commercially harvested in 1848 in Dungeness, a small fishing village on the Strait of Juan de Fuca on the Olympic Peninsula, perhaps the oldest commercial fishery on the West Coast.

Each year the Dungeness Crab Festival features crab in all its culinary variations, as well as a crabbing competition. Tagged crabs worth prizes are released off the Port Angeles pier.

Crabs grow larger by growing a new soft skin underneath their hard shell, then splitting along a seam and backing out of the old shell. Pumping water into the new shell stretches it out about an inch over the discarded shell.

Dungeness crabs dine on clams, smaller crabs, shrimp—basically anything they can catch. They prefer fresh meat, which is why fresh bait catches more crabs than rotten bait. In turn, octopus, large fish, and wolf eels prey on Dungeness.

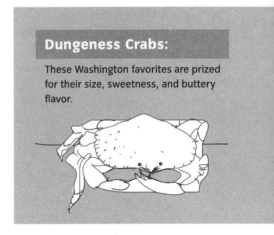

Dungeness Crabs:

These Washington favorites are prized for their size, sweetness, and buttery flavor.

Scary-looking claws and quick movements in any direction are good defenses, but a Dungeness crab can also bury its bulk in sand or mud and likes to hide in eelgrass beds.

A Dungeness has a grayish-brown shell with purple tinges and white-tipped claws. It's most abundant in the Puget Sound north of Seattle, with the bulk of the harvest coming from the Blaine and Point Roberts areas.

Crabbers quickly learn how to pick up a Dungeness, whose long claws can reach pretty far back. If one of those claws grabs a finger . . .

While East Coasters steam blue crabs, Washingtonians boil Dungeness crabs with saltwater (or salted water) and vinegar before engaging in culinary nirvana, proving that even mutant crabs taste great.

you know you're in
washington when...
... a spit sets a record

The longest natural sand spit in the United States sticks out 5 miles into the Strait of Juan de Fuca, off the north end of the Olympic Peninsula near Sequim.

The spit has slowly increased its length about 15 feet a year for more than a century, thanks to a combination of eroding bluffs, winds, currents, waves, and the Dungeness River flowing into Dungeness Bay, which is partly protected by the spit.

Dungeness Spit even has an offspring—Graveyard Spit, a finger of sand that points back toward the peninsula.

Thanks to the protective, northeast-curving Dungeness Spit, Dungeness Harbor and Dungeness Bay are protected from the surf and ripe with life in the tideflats and estuary. Denizens include crabs, clams, and oysters; shorebirds from phalaropes to turnstones; harbor seals; and young salmon and steelhead.

In 1915 the 756-acre Dungeness National Wildlife Refuge was created to protect wintering black brant and other migratory birds. More than 90 species nest in the refuge, including the northern pygmy owl and the willow flycatcher.

The northern side of the spit is open to hikers, but much of the rest is often off-limits to humans. Near the end of the spit is the New Dungeness Lighthouse, built in 1857 and one of the first lighthouses authorized by Congress for the West Coast.

The last full-time keeper left in 1994, but the New Dungeness Light Station Association agreed to maintain and operate the automated lighthouse with volunteers. These people pay to stay at the lighthouse in one-week shifts (starting each Saturday at low tide, which might occur in the middle of the night) and give tours to visitors.

Despite the fact that lighthouse access is limited to those who arrive via small boats or on foot, about 35,000 people have made the trip since 1994.

The state's other long stretch of sand is the Long Beach Peninsula in southwest Washington, which claims to be the world's longest beach (28 miles) open to vehicles.

Dungeness Spit:

The country's longest natural sand spit is home to varied fish and wildlife and a historic lighthouse.

you know you're in
washington when...
...entrepreneurial spirits thrive

Although most of the state's major corporate all-stars in the last 20 years have relied on technology, their predecessors were successful without software.

James Casey, 19, borrowed $100 in 1907 and started a messenger company in Seattle. Two years later UPS expanded and was on its way to becoming the world's largest package-delivery company.

Teenager John Nordstrom co-founded Nordstrom's in 1901, a Seattle shoe company legendary for customer service. The largest independent shoe chain in the nation expanded into clothing. It still has one rule for its employees: "Use your good judgment in all situations. There will be no additional rules." The Nordstrom family brought the Seahawks franchise to Seattle.

Eddie Bauer started in 1920 with a downtown Seattle store. The outdoorsman later spent $25 on goose down and material and created the first quilted insulated jacket on his way to becoming a force in the outdoor clothing market.

Twenty-three Pacific Northwest mountain climbers founded Recreational Equipment Inc. (REI), a consumer cooperative for climbing gear, in 1938. Today, REI is the nation's largest consumer co-op, with 2.8 million members. Its flagship store in Seattle includes a 65-foot climbing wall and a mountain-bike test trail.

The first Costco warehouse store opened in Seattle in 1983. The firm hit $3 billion in sales in less than six years, the first company to do so.

As for those high-tech wizards: Wireless pioneer and Centralia native Craig McCaw created McCaw Communications, the largest cellular company in the nation, in the 1980s. He sold it to AT&T for $13 billion. Jeff Bezos founded Amazon.com in a Bellevue garage. The digital strip mall survived against all odds to lead the Internet commerce world. And ex-Microsoft executive Rob Glaser started Progressive Networks in Seattle to provide progressive programming for the Web. The dream morphed into RealNetworks, which developed RealAudio, RealVideo, and RealPlayer.

Three other major companies (Boeing, Starbucks, and Microsoft) with Washington roots have their own entries in this book; see pages 5, 15, and 49, respectively.

Entrepreneurs:

Washington natives have found success with clothing, climbing gear, cellular service, digital strip malls, and streaming video, among other products.

24

you know you're in
washington when...
... music is the experience

Billionaire Paul Allen's passion for Jimi Hendrix turned into the world's largest collection of the Seattle-born musician's paraphernalia. Naturally Allen wanted a cool place to share it with the public, so he built the Experience Music Project (EMP).

Hendrix is honored in a love-it-or-hate-it building at the Seattle Center. Think of a swoopy Hendrix-shattered Fender Stratocaster. Think vibrant purple, red, silver, pale blue, and gold on the exterior, all colors representing songs and moments from rock history, including Hendrix's "Purple Haze." Think 21,000 individually shaped metal tiles affixed to the exterior of the building.

Although Allen's love of Hendrix sparked the concept, Allen and his sister, Jody Patton, soon expanded the goal from a Hendrix monument to a celebration of rock 'n' roll, with more than 80,000 items that reflect rock's roots and energy.

EMP can be a musical immersion for the eyes, ears, and hands. The world-class collection follows the progress of America's most rebellious music, from one of the first electric guitars to handwritten song sheets and high-tech recording studios. But it also extends to blues, jazz, hip-hop, country, funk, and punk.

Eric Clapton's "Brownie" guitar, a 1956 Fender Stratocaster made famous by the guitar anthem "Layla," is on display at EMP,

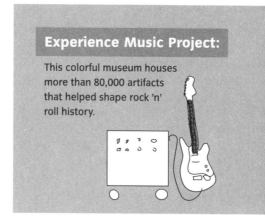

Experience Music Project: This colorful museum houses more than 80,000 artifacts that helped shape rock 'n' roll history.

along with Grandmaster Flash's Technics SL-1200 turntables, the Wheels of Steel that he used to help invent hip-hop. You can also see lyrics handwritten by Kurt Cobain and more artifacts from Nirvana, Soundgarden, Pearl Jam, and other bands that created the Seattle Sound of the 1980s and 1990s.

A psychedelic dandy outfit from Hendrix, sequined jacket and jeweled glove from Michael Jackson, "Goodbye Yellow Brick Road" costume from Elton John, and fringed shawl from Stevie Nicks are all part of the show. The *Roots and Branches* sculpture features more than 500 musical instruments and 30 computers. Also check out Sound Lab, where you can learn to play a hit guitar lick or mix a record.

Who knows? You could start a new musical genre and secure your own place at EMP.

Twenty-eight ferries and 20 ports of call make Washington State Ferries the largest ferry fleet in the United States. The fleet serves Puget Sound but extends to the San Juan Islands and Victoria, British Columbia, Canada.

The most popular tourist attraction in the state is both blessed and cursed by its 26 million passengers: The system allows many to live away from major cities yet ferry into work, but long waits during peak tourist weekends strain their patience.

Passengers usually are delivered without mishap. Occasionally, ferries run aground or take out a dock. They're more likely, however, to participate in a rescue effort in bone-chilling waters. (In 2004 a canine named Ruben jumped overboard. His owner grabbed a life ring and dove in after him. The ferry stopped, backed up, and dispatched a lifeboat to bring them back aboard.)

Once out on the water, your view might include the Seattle or Tacoma skyline, the Cascades and Olympics, the volcanic peaks of Mount Rainier or Mount Baker, tanker traffic, or the mostly wooded San Juan Islands. On some routes there's a chance to see a pod of black-and-white orcas.

Ferrying folks around Puget Sound dates back to the early 1900s, when private companies moved passengers using small steamboats dubbed the Mosquito Fleet. In

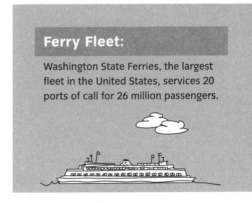

Ferry Fleet:

Washington State Ferries, the largest fleet in the United States, services 20 ports of call for 26 million passengers.

1951 the state bought the last ferry company, intending to run the boats as a temporary measure until bridges were built across the Sound. But legislators refused to fund the bridge project, and the state has owned the system ever since.

The 11 classes of ferries range from the Jumbo Mark II class (460 feet long, accommodating 218 vehicles and 2,500 passengers) to the high-speed Skagit/Kalama class (112 feet long, accommodating no vehicles but 250 passengers).

Except for the *Evergreen State* and the *Rhododendron,* Washington ferries have been named after Native American tribes or tribal words. These boats include the *Puyallup,* which means "generous people" in the Puyallup language; *Walla Walla,* Nez Perce for "place of many waters"; and *Hyak,* Chinook jargon for "fast or speedy" (of which it is neither).

you know you're in
washington when...
... the bridges are floating

Washington not only had the first floating bridge, but also boasts the three longest floating bridges on Earth. Of course, two of them have sunk, much to the chagrin of engineers and taxpayers. (But not the point.)

Residents have difficulty settling on the names of the two bridges that cross Lake Washington, connecting Seattle with the suburbs. Governor Albert D. Rosellini Bridge, the longest floating bridge in the world (7,578 feet), is also called the 520 Bridge for the highway designation, and the Evergreen Point Bridge. Lacey V. Murrow Memorial Bridge (6,620 feet) is also called the I–90 Bridge, Lake Washington Floating Bridge, and Mercer Island Bridge.

Our third floater is the 6,521-foot-long Hood Canal Bridge. It opened in 1961, conquering significant depths and tidal swings but not the 80- to 120-mile-per-hour winds in 1979 that created 10- to 15-foot waves. The pounding sank more than half the pontoons in less than an hour. Mother Nature wasn't the only culprit; workers had left open pontoon access hatches, allowing water to pour in. The western half of the bridge was rebuilt and reopened to traffic in October 1982.

The I–90 Bridge suffered a similar fate. The 1.25-mile, 25-pontoon bridge originally opened in 1940, completing the interstate's 3,111-mile link between Boston and Seattle. (Technically, the twin spans could be counted as two bridges, but we have enough trouble with names, so let's not go there.)

Traffic exceeded expectations. Rural Bellevue, which to that time hadn't seen anything more exciting than raccoons in the chicken houses, grew into the state's fourth largest city; Mercer Island became a bedroom community to Seattle.

In 1990 the span was closed for a $35.6 million renovation. A combination of large holes cut into the pontoons for access, hatchways left open (yes, you've heard that one before), and a week of rain and high winds caused eight pontoons to break apart and sink about 300 feet on November 25. (The current bridge was erected in 1993.)

Countless people witnessed the dive because the relatively slow process allowed television crews to broadcast the transportation disaster.

Floating Bridges:

The world's three longest pontoon bridges cross Lake Washington and Hood Canal.

The self-proclaimed Center of the Universe is Seattle's most eclectic neighborhood. The Republic of Fremont once declared its independence from Seattle, but no shots were fired.

Fremont has a trio of edgy artworks, but the least quirky is the most cared for in the city. The Interurban sculpture shows five people and a dog under a shelter, patiently waiting for the light-rail that no longer runs to downtown. The statue inspires sometimes artistically mischievous residents to dress up the riders, celebrating causes, holidays, and university teams.

A statue of Lenin has a home in Fremont, too. Slavic artist Emil Venkov ditched the idea of a traditional Lenin; instead, his Lenin is surrounded by flames and guns. The seven-ton statue was toppled in Poprad, Slovakia, during the 1989 revolution that broke up the Soviet Union.

Lewis Carpenter, an American teaching in Poprad, mortgaged his house and brought Lenin back to the United States. If a statue of a dictator would look good in your yard, this is your lucky day. It's for sale. Meanwhile, Fremont claims it as as proof that art outlives politics.

For the really peculiar, walk under the Aurora Bridge and stand in awe of the 18-foot Fremont troll crushing a Volkswagen

Beetle in one hand. Don't get too close, though. He looks very hungry.

Fremont residents debated what would be the proper landmark for the Center of the Universe (an anonymously donated sign at Fremont Avenue and North 34th Street marks the spot) before settling on a dismantled 1950s Cold War rocket fuselage.

Eventually the 53-foot structure was erected, with the community declaring the rocket its armed forces, complete with a Fremont family crest that incorporates the local motto: *De libertas quirkas* (roughly translated, "Freedom to be peculiar").

Oh, and about that Center of the Universe thing? The King County Council actually declared that Fremont is the Center of the Universe.

Fremont:

Seattle's artistically eccentric neighborhood is known for its VW-eating troll and statue of Vladimir Lenin.

you know you're in
washington when...
... apples, sweet cherries, and pears are number one

Cherries are an aphrodisiac? Now that we have your attention, let us reveal that Washington is famous for its Rainier cherries, a yellow-skinned, red-blush variety resulting from crossbreeding Bing and Van varieties.

The state grows 57 percent of all U.S. cherries, which are also a hit overseas. Taiwan's recording stars have been filmed wandering state orchards to promote cherries as a sensuous and hip foreign luxury.

As to their popularity, B. J. Thurlby, president of the Northwest Cherry Growers in Yakima, has an opinion: "While cherries have always been a sensual fruit, I've had more than a few consumers tell me over the years that Rainier cherries have some sort of aphrodisiac effect. We would have liked to have conducted some scientific studies to confirm this, but we were worried that we'd have way too many volunteers for the focus group."

Another fruit that originally grew in Kazakhstan and spread east along the Silk Road has turned into Washington's largest agricultural product: apples. State orchards yield almost 60 percent of U.S. apples—10 to 12 billion apples, all picked by hand.

The classic Red Delicious is the main variety, accounting for more than one-third of the crop. Washington also produces about two-thirds of the U.S. organic crop. Afi-

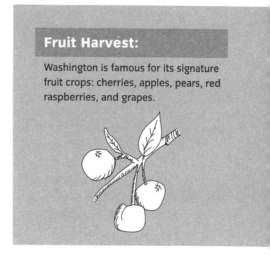

Fruit Harvest:

Washington is famous for its signature fruit crops: cherries, apples, pears, red raspberries, and grapes.

cionados celebrate the fruit with the state's oldest major festival, the Washington State Apple Blossom Festival in Wenatchee.

Buying a box of Aplets and Cotlets has been a Washington tradition since 1920. These sweets, made from apples (or apricots) and walnuts, were introduced in 1920. The original recipe from Liberty Orchards in Cashmere calls for the fruit to be slow-cooked to a smooth puree, blended with English walnuts, and rolled in powdered sugar.

As for other fruits, Washington produces almost 50 percent of pears and 91 percent of red raspberries grown in the United States. It also grows more Concord and Niagara grapes than any other state in the nation.

29

you know you're in
washington when...
... a bridge becomes a roller coaster

The third-longest suspension bridge in the world, the 5,939-foot-long Tacoma Narrows Bridge, opened on July 1, 1940. The pride of Washington was reflected in a nearby bank billboard: as secure as the new narrows bridge.

It was designed by a state engineer but modified by renowned suspension bridge engineer Leon Moisseiff, who replaced open (for wind passage) stiffening trusses with solid plate girders.

During construction, however, the road bed rippled even in slight winds. Some motion-sick workers chewed on lemons, but engineers said not to worry. Locals nicknamed the bridge Galloping Gertie; thousands drove to Tacoma to ride the undulations of the 2,800-foot center span, sometimes losing sight of vehicles in front of them.

Hydraulic buffers and tie-down cables were added, but wind-tunnel tests indicated that a twisting motion was still possible. Repair recommendations included cutting holes in the solid girders or adding wind deflectors.

On November 7, 1940, the bridge deck began to heave in 35–42 mile per hour winds. Just before the bridge closed at 10:00 A.M., local newspaper editor Leonard Coatsworth and his daughter's spaniel, Tubby, rode onto the span. The undulation quickly went from 5- to 28-foot waves; the

Galloping Gertie:

This suspension bridge acted like a roller coaster before twisting and collapsing into the Tacoma Narrows in 1940.

roadbed tilted up 45 degrees one way, then the other. Coatsworth lost control of his car but managed to crawl out and run off the bridge.

Concrete was falling by 10:30 A.M. Bolts sheered, cables snapped and flew through the air, and steel shrieked and wailed. At 11:02 A.M. a 600-foot section of the center span fell into the water, followed by a rain of bridge parts, vehicles, and one spaniel. By 11:10 the most dramatic failure in bridge history was over.

The bridge was replaced in 1950 by Sturdy Gertie. In 2007 a new bridge will parallel the existing one. For more than 50 years no U.S. suspension bridge has been erected without passing wind tunnel tests.

you know you're in
washington when...
...your college fight song is about geoducks

Puget Sound is home to the highest density of geoducks in the mainland United States. The state's most profitable shellfish is also the world's largest burrowing clam. An average geoduck weighs less than 3 pounds, but the Seattle Aquarium once had a 13-pounder.

Although it is spelled geoduck, the name is pronounced "GOO-wee-duck." It comes from a Lushootseed phrase meaning "dig deep." A young geoduck digs down 3 feet in its first three years of life and stays there, living up to 140 years off Puget Sound's phytoplankton menu.

The white oblong shell contains rings representing each year of growth, about 1 inch a year in shell length for a few years, then much less after that.

A newcomer can't help but think of male anatomy when sighting a geoduck, which features an elastic, phallic siphon up to 39 inches long—too long to fit in its shell. Less suggestive minds might picture an elephant's trunk!

When clammers walk on the beach at low tide, geoducks sense the vibrations and withdraw their siphons, the compression shooting seawater several feet in the air and giving away their location. Its small foot and large size don't allow for a fast getaway, so a digger armed with an open-ended metal tube can force it down around a clam, then dig out the sand by hand.

Successful diggers often boil and skin the neck, then chop the meat for chowder. Some swear it's better than abalone.

Private diggers must wait for extreme low tides to hunt geoducks. Commercial divers harvest the clams in deeper water and then rush them to Asian markets, where a plate of geoducks sells for about $60.

And that fight song? The mascot of Evergreen State College in Olympia is the geoduck, thus "The Geoduck Fight Song," written by Malcolm Stilson in 1971. Sing the chorus in your waders, and see if you don't get into the spirit, too.

> Go, Geoducks go,
> Through the mud and the sand, let's go.
> Siphon high, squirt it out,
> Swivel all about, let it all hang out.

Geoduck:

The most profitable shellfish in Washington, this creature lives below the sand of Puget Sound.

Ginkgo Petrified Forest State Park in Vantage is one of the world's most unusual fossil forests, with about 200 species of petrified wood and plants.

Looking at the shrub-covered landscape today, it's tough to imagine it blanketed with deciduous and conifer forests some 16 million years ago, before volcanic eruptions covered the humid land in ash and lava. Floods swept across the eastern two-thirds of the state about 15,000 years ago, eroding the basalt (solidified lava) flows and exposing petrified logs. The 7,470-acre state park was created after a construction crew discovered the fossil forest in 1927.

Wood becomes petrified in a two-step process: First, the wood is covered sufficiently to keep out oxygen and prevent decay. Volcanic ash, lava flows, or flood sediments can provide this condition. Then minerals (mainly silica) dissolved in groundwater seep into the wood. A chemical process preserves the cell structure and turns once-living species into trees of stone. Different colors are a result of other minerals staining the wood.

Petrified wood is the official gemstone of Washington. Ginkgo State Park's namesake is a bridge to the distant past, a living fossil native to China. Its distinctive leaf resembles a partly opened fan. While fossilized ginkgo leaves have been found around the world, it's rare to find fossilized wood. In fact, only a few of the thousands of petrified trees in the park are ginkgo, once extinct in North America.

Other tree species in the park include teak, fir, redwood, madrona, swamp cypress, oak, and witch hazel. What's particularly unusual about this gathering is that many of these trees are from different climate zones. How they all came to be in the same general location is not known.

Walk the 1.5-mile Trees of Stone Interpretive Trail to see 22 examples of petrified logs. If you keep an eye on the hills, you might spot a bighorn sheep or two. The state park is also home to about 60 petroglyphs salvaged from basalt cliffs when the Wanapum Dam was built on the Columbia River in the 1950s.

Ginkgo Petrified Forest State Park:

Petrified wood is the official gemstone of Washington, and this state park in Vantage has plenty of it.

washington when...

...glaciers eat rocks

For a close encounter of the fascinating kind, chill out at the toe (snout) of one of Washington's many glaciers. The state has about 70 percent of the glaciers in the mainland United States.

In the Lower 48, Carbon Glacier flows to the lowest altitude of any glacier; 4.3-square-mile Emmons Glacier is the largest; and at 700 feet deep, Carbon Glacier has the greatest thickness and volume. All are located in Mount Rainier National Park.

Rivers of ice are found in the Cascade and Olympic mountain ranges. Unlike many glaciers in Alaska that creep to the shoreline and break off into the water (a process called calving), Washington's glaciers are confined to land.

From a distance their surfaces look smooth and stable. Up close reality sets in. Glaciers are in constant motion. Once compressed ice reaches about 60 feet thick, its sheer weight forces shape changes, often creating giant crevasses hundreds of feet long and hundreds of feet deep.

The top of a glacier moves quicker than the bottom because the latter experiences resistance with the ground. That friction grinds down and chews up rocks and soil, often carrying the debris along in dark bands called moraines.

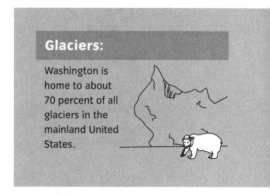

Glaciers:

Washington is home to about 70 percent of all glaciers in the mainland United States.

As they move, glaciers creak, boom, rumble, crack, and groan. They advance and retreat as the ice melts or increases, a reflection of warmer and cooler temperatures. (Mount Rainier's Nisqually Glacier moved 29 inches per day in May 1970!) Melting glacier ice provides the state with 470 billion gallons of water each summer.

A 3,000-foot-deep glacier covered Seattle a mere 15,000 years ago. Its advance and retreat carved out the Puget Sound that exists today. About 35,000 years ago the Cowlitz-Ingraham Glacier flowed about 65 miles, nearly all the way to Mossyrock.

While many vistas offer good views, it's possible to safely hike to many glaciers. With proper equipment, training, and nerve, people climb the icy sides or walk across the glaciers, admiring their bluish hues and symphony of sound.

Few funeral processions have storylines that can match the Pickled Pioneer's tale.

Wilhelm Keil and his religious commune, the Bethelites, were packing for Washington Territory in 1855. Keil's 19-year-old son, Willie, was to lead the wagon train but died of malaria days before departing Missouri.

The German immigrant put him inside a lead-lined coffin filled with the 100-proof Golden Rule whiskey that the Bethelites distilled. The coffin was placed in a black-draped, wagon-turned-hearse. Willie led the 35-wagon, 250-person expedition, sloshing around in alcohol.

Many wagon trains were attacked by Native Americans. The Bethelites were stopped at least twice, but the leaders only had to point at the hearse; someone would open the coffin, and the Native Americans would look and ride away. Willie was buried along what is now Highway 6 between Raymond and Centralia. The area proved too wet, and the colony moved to Oregon.

Today, Willie's gravesite gets some attention from curious tourists. But other Washington graves draw visitors from around the world. Lake View Cemetery in Seattle has the most well-known residents, including Bruce Lee, who lived much of his life in the city, and his son Brandon, both martial arts experts and film actors.

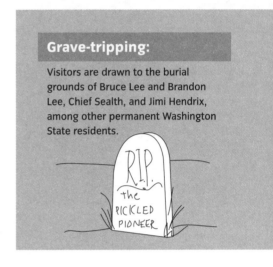

Grave-tripping:

Visitors are drawn to the burial grounds of Bruce Lee and Brandon Lee, Chief Sealth, and Jimi Hendrix, among other permanent Washington State residents.

Lake View is also home to Seattle's original movers and shakers (the Dennys, Hortons, Yeslers, and Maynards) and to Princess Angeline, daughter of the city's namesake, Chief Sealth. At her request she was buried near her friend, Henry Yesler. Sealth is buried in Suquamish; his monument includes a cross framed with dugout canoes.

When Nirvana's Kurt Cobain died, Lake View denied him a spot (citing the stream of visitors drawn by the Lees). Instead, Cobain has a bench in his honor near the Seattle home in which he died. Some of his ashes were scattered near a Buddhist monastery in New York and in the Wishkah River near his childhood home.

Rock guitar legend and Seattle high school graduate Jimi Hendrix is buried in Renton.

The Graveyard of the Pacific runs the length of the Washington coast and covers a bit of northwest Oregon and the west side of Vancouver Island. Almost 2,000 vessels and at least 700 lives have been lost there, most during fierce storms.

Ships from at least 10 countries have gone down, including warships, sternwheelers, fishing boats, schooners, and, if Native American legends are correct, a Chinese junk. Some shipwreck remains are still partly exposed on the beaches of Washington.

Many vessels wrecked near the mouth of the Columbia River, which has one of the most treacherous sandbars in the world. Even on a good day, crossing the Columbia Bar is a challenge: A powerful river meets an ocean to create a maelstrom of water; shifting sandbars and natural river channels can force ships to turn sideways to the currents, allowing waves and wind to take their toll.

A Spanish explorer first put the river on a chart in 1775; the British decided that the shoals were impassable and called the nearby headland Cape Disappointment. An American captain successfully crossed the bar in 1792.

Technology and bar pilots have reduced tragedies. The bar pilot tradition dates back to 1795, when a Chinook chief paddled his canoe and guided sailing ships through the shifting shallows.

Today, there are about 20 licensed Columbia River pilots who board ships to guide them across the bar. In 2006 one pilot drowned when he fell while transferring from a cargo ship to the pilot boat at night in 18-foot seas and 50-mile-per-hour winds.

Since 1865 a combination of volunteers (using salvaged and government-funded equipment) and paid crews of the U.S. Life-Saving Service (which in 1915 became the U.S. Coast Guard) have made thousands of rescues, piloting lifeboats through some of the roughest surf in the world.

Today's boats can roll in the surf and right themselves without major damage. Rescue crews, trained since 1980 at Ilwaco's National Motor Lifeboat School, still get plenty of practice; they receive 300 to 400 calls for help a year.

Graveyard of the Pacific:

Almost 2,000 vessels have been lost in this corridor, which runs the length of the Washington coast.

you know you're in
washington when...
...grunge is not a state of filth

The Melvins and Mudhoney played it on the underground circuit, but Nirvana and Pearl Jam picked up the Seattle Sound, put it on their backs, and carried it all the way to mainstream America.

Called grunge, this combination of hardcore rock and punk without theatrical touches is marked by distorted guitars, heavyweight drumming, and slower tempos. Although it is overloaded with angst, anger, and teenage disenchantment, it also delivers songs about prejudice and poverty.

Many credit the band Green River with originating the unruly genre in 1983. When the group split five years later, its members started Mother Love Bone and Mudhoney and inspired Soundgarden.

Nirvana and Pearl Jam arrived on the second wave of grunge, putting Seattle on the musical map and dominating the genre from 1991 to 1994. The turning point was Nirvana's number-one album, *Nevermind,* released in 1991. It contained the Generation X theme song "Smells Like Teen Spirit."

The movie *Singles* (1992), filmed in Seattle, added to national notice with cameo appearances from Pearl Jam, Alice in Chains, and Soundgarden. Soon grunge style (cheap clothes, flannel shirts, outdoorsy look) turned into high fashion. *Vanity Fair* even published a grunge fashion spread.

As Seattle bands scored big recording contracts, the musicians became celebrities. But commercialization cost the genre its heart. The major bands didn't want to write radio-friendly hooks for their labels, so the corporations found second-tier bands willing to cooperate. Grunge became slicker and a pale imitation of its original self.

The nail in the coffin, so to speak, was the suicide of Nirvana's Kurt Cobain. Some believe he was tired of bearing the burden of being called a spokesman for Generation X, and he was found dead of a self-inflicted gunshot wound in 1994. The grief of his fans mirrored that of the 1960s generation when John Lennon died.

Grunge:

Also called the Seattle Sound, this genre was inspired by punk and heavy metal, with heavy doses of nihilism.

Ivar Haglund was a 20th-century five-star character, the type that's noticeably absent now. Seattle's irreverent King of Clams created publicity stunts that turned his Acres of Clams restaurant into a must-stop for waterfront visitors.

Haglund, a folksinger who counted Woody Guthrie and Pete Seeger as friends, created Seattle's first aquarium in 1938 (it closed in 1956); started his now-famous waterfront eatery in 1946; began the "Fourth of Jul-Ivar" fireworks tradition in 1965; and in that same year bought Pier 54, becoming a "a member of the Elliott Bay pierage, a dock duke 54th in a line of piers!" In 1976 he bought Smith Tower, the city's oldest skyscraper.

No slick ad campaigns for Haglund. His brain worked overtime on pranks and stunts. He could get away with so much in part because his roots ran deep into Seattle soil: His maternal grandparents bought Alki Point from pioneer Doc Maynard.

In front of the aquarium, Haglund performed songs while sitting on a stool and wearing his trademark captain's hat. In 1940 he even dressed a seal in a pinafore and lace baby hat and took it to see a department store Santa Claus.

To promote his restaurant Haglund printed clam stamps, but the U.S. Post Office confiscated the stamps and plates. He was dubbed the Crown Prince of Corn when he

Haglund, Ivar:

Seattle's five-star character, aka Mayor of the Waterfront, ruled with clams, songs, and stunts.

rushed outside the eatery with a plate of pancakes and scooped up some of the syrup spilled from a railroad car.

In 1977 Haglund raised a 16-foot-long Rainbow Salmon windsock over Smith Tower, violating a municipal building code. The city protested but eventually gave in.

Haglund's quips were legendary; they included "Seafood is Brain Food. Be Wise at Ivar's" and his motto, "Keep Clam." He turned the "Old Settler's Song" into his theme song, thanks to these lines:

> No longer the slave of ambition
> I laugh at the world and its shams,
> As I think of my happy condition
> Surrounded by acres of clams.

In 1985 Haglund went to the Big Clam Acre in the Sky, but he is forever immortalized in local lore and as a bobblehead doll.

you know you're in
washington when...
...radioactivity means job security

The largest nuclear-waste dump in the Western Hemisphere—also the world's largest environmental clean-up site—sits in the southeast corner of the state. The Hanford Nuclear Reservation was home to the first operating plutonium reactor and provided radioactive material for Fat Man (the bomb dropped on Nagasaki, Japan) and for much of the U.S. nuclear weapons stockpile.

Started in 1943 as the Hanford Engineer Works (part of the Manhattan Project), the site covers 586 square miles, including a 50-mile stretch of the Columbia River. The federal government bought two towns and the surrounding farmland, evacuated everyone, and brought in about 50,000 workers and their families to develop weapons-grade plutonium. Nearby Richland's economic health has depended on Hanford since then.

During the reservation's very secret first 40 years, radioactive materials were vented into the air, and contaminates entered the land and the Columbia. About 53 million gallons of nuclear sludge were buried in tanks, some of which eventually started leaking. That sludge will be a danger for roughly 250,000 years.

Billions of dollars are being spent to clean up the controversial site, particularly the tanks, but many people are concerned that several radioactive plumes of groundwater are creeping toward the Columbia. More-

Hanford Nuclear Reservation:

This site in southeast Washington is the largest nuclear-waste dump in the Western Hemisphere.

over, a recent study found an increase in thyroid disease in men who lived next to Hanford decades ago, when radioactive iodine was released into the air.

Also tied to the past is Richland High School, which in 1945 changed its mascot from the Beavers to the Bombers, with a mushroom cloud as part of the logo. Administrators defend the choice by saying that the name actually refers to a B-17 bomber that Hanford workers paid to have built for the Army Air Force in 1944. But there's no escaping the symbolism of the mushroom cloud, and it's possible to buy a 10-inch wooden bomb as an RHS souvenir.

Another questionable name is the Atomic Cup, a hydroplane race hosted by the tri-cities of Richland, Kennewick, and Pasco since 1965.

you know you're in
washington when...
... your neighborhood is floating

"Houseboats are to Seattle what cable cars are to San Francisco," says houseboat resident and Discover Houseboating tour guide Jeri Callahan.

Seattle has the most houseboats moored to docks connected to sewer systems in the nation—nearly 500 along the shores of Lake Union and Portage Bay. They range from one-roomers to *Architectural Digest*–style creations, all exuding a certain romance. While most are older, modest homes on cedar logs, others are new with two stories, ferro-cement floats, and basements.

Houseboats have been on Lake Union since before 1900, when residents were mainly fishermen and dock workers who lashed together logs and built shacks on top. In the early 1900s, construction to join Lake Union with Puget Sound drew workers who needed cheap housing. They built more floating shanties.

By the Depression there were about 2,000 houseboats in Seattle. Eventually Lake Union was "civilized." Residents pressured politicians to clean up the polluted lake (ergo the sewers). Some say those living on the hillsides with views of the lake wanted the floating eyesores to be gone.

With sewer lines running along the shore, property values increased. Moorage fees rose, and many houseboats were evicted. Some houseboats showed up on beaches; others were sold as salvage, were towed away, or found new homes when dock owners lengthened their docks to accommodate some of the displaced houseboats.

The evictions led to a 1984 moorage rent-control ordinance. The consequence was that houseboat values soared. Most of the once-eclectic mix of fiercely independent houseboat owners eventually lost out to rising prices and dock fees.

Callahan says that her "shack on a raft" (600 square feet and built before 1928) is worth about $300,000. Moorage at a new dock that can handle the larger, two-story floating homes costs about $700,000, pushing the total cost of houseboat ownership over the $1 million mark, a far cry from a floating shantytown.

Houseboats:

On Lake Union and Portage Bay, high-priced floating homes have replaced shanties on log rafts.

Mention Native Americans in the 21st century, and casinos might spring to mind. But Washington tribes that survived wars, loss of land, and broken treaties have much more than gambling to offer.

Although the Tulalip Tribes near Marysville run a casino, they also own the successful Quil Ceda Village Business Park and a cablevision company.

The White River Amphitheater, located on the Muckleshoot Indian Reservation, draws well-known musicians during the summer. The Yakama Nation in central Washington has its own Cultural Heritage Center. And the Makah Museum in Neah Bay is often recognized as the best small museum in Washington and the finest tribal museum in the United States.

Many tribes participate in celebrations open to the public. In Seattle an annual powwow is held at Discovery Park's Daybreak Star Cultural Center, home of the United Indians of All Tribes Foundation. The center is located on what was once Fort Lawton, a military base scheduled for surplus that Native American activists invaded in 1970 in an effort to gain some of the land. Eventually they secured 20 acres as a cultural site.

For hundreds of thousands of visitors a year, however, the cultural learning moment is packed into a couple of hours at Tillicum Village at Blake Island State Park, an 8-mile boat ride from downtown Seattle. Legend says that the former Suquamish camping ground was the birthplace of Chief Sealth, for whom Seattle was named.

Tillicum Village (styled after a huge cedar longhouse) was started in 1962 by non-Indian Bill Hewitt to celebrate the Northwest Coast native culture with salmon dinners, crafts, ceremonial dances, songs, and storytelling. The salmon is cooked on cedar stakes over open alder fires. The staff, which represents several Northwest Coast Indian tribes, has served such luminaries as President Clinton and Norway's King Olaf.

Indian Culture:

Native American tribes across the state celebrate their heritage, with two especially popular public events held in Seattle and at Blake Island State Park.

you know you're in
washington when...
... peace is given a chance

It's not often that you can stand with your feet in two countries, but it's doable at Peace Arch State Park in Blaine, where the beautiful International Peace Arch honors peaceful relations between Canada and the United States.

The arch straddles the border between Blaine and Surrey, British Columbia, at the longest undefended boundary in the world and the third-busiest crossing on the U.S. border with Canada.

The 67-foot white arch commemorates the centennial of the signing of the Treaty of Ghent, which ended the War of 1812 between Great Britain and the United States.

Hundreds of thousands of visitors stop to enjoy the park gardens and read the inscriptions on the arch. The American side of the first monument dedicated to world peace bears the words CHILDREN OF A COMMON MOTHER; on the Canadian side is the phrase BRETHREN DWELLING TOGETHER IN UNITY; and inside the portal are the words MAY THESE GATES NEVER BE CLOSED. Bronze gates are hinged on either side of the border, symbolizing that both countries would have to declare the border closed in order to close the gates.

Fragments of the *Mayflower* and the Canadian steamship *Beaver* were sealed in the walls during the arch's 1921 dedication.

Washington's railroad- and road-building

International Peace Arch:

This graceful arch is anchored in U.S. and Canadian soil on the longest undefended boundary in the world.

millionaire pacifist Sam Hill gets credit for envisioning the Peace Arch. Schoolchildren collected pennies and nickels to fund it, Victoria's R. P. Butchart (of Butchart Gardens) donated 3,500 sacks of concrete, and New Yorker E. H. Gary (of the U.S. Steel Corporation) donated 50 tons of steel.

But like a good capitalist, Hill also wanted a resort and golf course to bring in money that would match his community spirit. Prohibition stopped most Americans from drinking outside the home, so Hill built a resort that Washington residents could easily reach—across the border in Canada, where liquor was legal.

The Semiahmoo Club opened in 1927 and did well until Prohibition ended in 1933. The Peace Portal Golf Course remains open.

41

Imagine a dilapidated 276-foot Airstream trailer set on a hull, or a silver bullet with portholes. You've just pictured the *Kalakala*, a Puget Sound icon on the National Register of Historic Places.

The star-crossed people-carrier started in 1926 as a California steamship, the *Peralta*. In 1927 ballast shifted and five people fell overboard and drowned; six years later fire destroyed the superstructure. The Black Ball Line bought the remains, and a tug delivered it to the Lake Washington Shipyard. Turned into a ferry with a radically streamlined shape wrapped in aluminum, it became the world's only art deco ferry.

Renamed the *Kalakala* ("flying bird" in Chinook), the vessel launched in 1935 with 100,000 people watching. For 32 years thereafter it ferried millions of passengers.

When Pearl Harbor was bombed, Bremerton Navy Yard worked around the clock. The *Kalakala* carried as many as 5,000 shipyard workers and sailors per trip and earned the nickname "The Workhorse of Puget Sound." Over the years the *Kalakala* collided with another ferry, rammed a barge (knocking two railroad cars into Puget Sound), rammed its own dock, and rammed the new ferry terminal in Seattle.

A new *Kalakala* era began in 1967. The vessel was sold, towed to Alaska, and converted into a crab-processing plant; several

The *Kalakala:*

This historic ferry holds a piece of Puget Sound's history and heart.

bankruptcies and sales followed.

Sculptor Pete Bevis saw the *Kalakala* in 1984. Fascinated by its elegant curves, he later created a nonprofit foundation to rescue the ferry, and the *Kalakala* returned to Seattle in 1998. Long on dreams and short on cash, the Kalakala Foundation board planned to turn the vessel into an art deco–era museum. But three proposals for permanent moorage in Seattle were turned down, and bankruptcy drove another sale.

In 2004 the *Kalakala* was towed to Neah Bay in the far northwest corner of the state. Differences quickly developed with the Makah Tribal Council, and the ferry was sent packing once more—this time to Tacoma, where there's a chance for a permanent home and a $15 million restoration.

you know you're in
washington when...
...skeletal remains become a federal case

Millions of Americans have at least a casual interest in their genealogical roots. But one skeleton found in Washington State took ancestral ties to court.

Native Americans call him the Ancient One; scientists call him Kennewick Man. The 9,000-year-old skeleton was found along the Columbia River in 1996 near Kennewick by two hydroplane race spectators.

History, religion, science, public policy, and tribal rights quickly collided, as is often the case when ancient remains are found. Historically, archeologists engaged in grave-robbing when it came to nonwhite skeletal remains. In the 1970s many tribes rebelled against that approach. Eventually the American Graves Protection and Repatriation Act was passed to protect cultural claims.

Shortly after the Kennewick Man was found, the Umatilla, Yakama, Nez Perce, Wanapum, and Colville tribes wanted to rebury the skeleton. They claimed to be related to the Ancient One because he was uncovered on their traditional homeland; their religious beliefs said that reburial was necessary. Scientists wanted to study the skeleton, one of the oldest and most complete to be discovered in North America. They argued that a link between modern Indians and the Kennewick Man could not be proven.

The federal government initially sided with the tribes. For eight years the two sides battled it out in courtrooms and in the court of public opinion. In 2004 a federal appeals court ruled that the skeleton was too ancient to be linked to the tribes and that scientists could proceed.

Since then scientists have studied the 350 bone fragments with high-resolution scans, carbon dating, isotopic studies, and DNA analysis. They say that the skull is not similar to those of Northwest tribe members, leaving open the possibility that Kennewick Man's ancestors migrated from Asia about 11,000 years ago.

This theory contradicts tribal oral histories that say Native American people have been here since the dawn of time. The tribes say that trying to prove differently is a way of turning Native Americans into just another immigrant people.

Kennewick Man:

The 9,000-year-old skeleton may help determine who the original North American inhabitants were.

you know you're in
washington when...
... polka music reigns

Dropping out of 4,061-foot Stevens Pass, State Route 2 parallels the Wenatchee River on its twisting way through scenic Tumwater Canyon to a big-hearted small town nestled below towering snow-covered peaks.

Welcome to Leavenworth, the little central Washington town that transformed itself from one staggered by lack of economic opportunities when the mill closed and the railroad left to an imitation Bavarian town in the Alps.

About two million visitors a year are testimony to the success of Project Alpine. Starting in 1965, businesses remodeled their buildings, residents donned Bavarian-style costumes, and Bavarian-themed gift shops and restaurants opened. Festivals soon followed: Autumn Leaf, Christmas Lighting, Maifest, Oktoberfest, Accordion.

A Leavenworth festival is a good excuse to explore the local nutcracker museum, marvel at beer steins and Bavarian wax sculptures, admire the cuckoo clocks, listen to polka music, follow the beer wagon, and watch German dances on the street.

Stock up for Christmas at Kris Kringl, two floors of Christmas ornamentation; or browse Die Musik Box's 4,000 items. Be sure to stop at Gustav's Onion Dome Restaurant, a landmark. Eat a Gustav burger and hot sauerkraut, and check out the antique skiing and ice-skating equipment. The original copper dome was removed after a 1990 fire but rebuilt.

Or eat at King Ludwig's Restaurant, famous for its schweinshax'n. The owners think they prepare more pork hocks, Bavarian style, than any other restaurant west of Chicago. Imported German beers are on tap, all in accordance with the German Purity Law of 1516, which stipulates that only the natural ingredients of barley, malt, hops, yeast, and brewing water may be used.

These days wine-tasting shops are edging in, reflecting the state's booming wine industry. The town packages all the elements and delivers it in *gemütlichkeit* style: with friendliness and congeniality.

Leavenworth:

Financially desperate residents turned this town into an illusion of a Bavarian Alps village.

you know you're in
washington when...
...you can rent history

Forget the little house on the prairie and Thoreau's cabin in the woods. In Washington, history, romance, and a good night's sleep are but a credit card away. Rent a fire lookout, a lighthouse, or historic officers' quarters, and get a taste of "back then."

Lookouts often are primitive accommodations, and those perched on long posts might rock a little in a stiff wind at the top of the mountain. Nonetheless, it's hard to beat the views and star-studded skies away from civilization's light pollution.

None of the lookouts is more than 14-by-14 feet because the packhorses that carried the building materials couldn't manage longer boards. But you won't spend a lot of money for a room with a view. The $40-a-night Evergreen Mountain lookout, located near Skykomish at an elevation of 5,587 feet, offers a good look at a 10,541-foot volcano, Glacier Peak. The 1935 lookout has been restored and is on the National Register of Historic Places.

You can expect few amenities once you've hiked in 1.5 miles and gained 1,300 feet in elevation. The outhouse is several hundred feet down the ridge, so plan ahead and take a flashlight with fresh batteries.

Clearwater Lookout Cabin in the Umatilla National Forest, also built in 1935, sits at the base of a 94-foot closed lookout at 5,600 feet elevation. It comes with a heater,

Lookouts:

Vacationers can rent one of these U.S. Forest Service cabins—or spend a little more on the former residence of a lighthouse keeper or military officer.

cook stove, and refrigerator (all powered by propane) for $25 a night.

History costs more near sea level. Cape Disappointment State Park (formerly Fort Canby State Park) offers the head lighthouse keeper's quarters from $178 on off-season weeknights to $355 a night during the summer. The two-story Victorian–era residence has a view of the top third of the lighthouse and the Pacific Ocean. High ceilings and hardwood floors are features of the period-furnished living room, grand dining room, and library.

At Fort Worden State Park, you can rest near a shoreline bluff in a former Victorian home ($111 to $360 a night) built for officers and their families or choose to rent The Castle, the oldest building at the fort.

45

Lye is an important ingredient in soap making. Turns out it's also handy for . . . fish preparation?

Ya sure, you betcha! Lutefisk (translation: "lye fish") is white fish that has been skinned, salted and dried, and then soaked in lye to pull out the salt to make it marginally more edible—if a whitish gray gelatinous mass can be considered edible.

Apparently it is to Scandinavians, who once considered lutefisk a dietary staple. (In the olden days it got them through those long, cold winter months). Immigrants brought this culinary tradition to America in the late 19th and early 20th centuries. Many of them settled in Seattle. By 1910 about one-third of the city's immigrants hailed from Norway, Sweden, Finland, and Denmark.

Most of those newcomers headed to the Ballard neighborhood, at which point lutefisk consumption dropped precipitously. But their descendants celebrate their heritage each July with the Ballard Seafood Fest and a lutefisk-eating contest. The winner gets cash, which can be used for remedies to cure whatever malady compelled him or her to ingest lutefisk in the first place.

If you're intrigued, head over to Poulsbo the third Saturday of October for the lutefisk and lefse dinner at First Lutheran Church, which has sponsored the fund-

Lutefisk:

This Scandinavian "delicacy"—dried white fish that has been soaked in lye—is celebrated in Seattle.

raising bash since 1912. Expect more than 2,000 pounds of lutefisk and 2,000 pieces of lefse, a flat unleavened Scandinavian bread.

Some Scandinavian descendants claim to actually like lutefisk, but listen closely for the fine print: "I eat it only once a year." Even their kin back in the motherland usually save it for the winter holiday season.

If you miss the chance to buy lutefisk, you can make it at home. Just be careful, as all white fish are not created equal. Pollack and haddock are almost odorless—a good thing when you consider the pungent smell of lye—but cod has a strong odor on its own.

Ya sure, you betcha!

you know you're in
washington when...
...campsites are reserved for paddlers

Washington sea kayakers used to face a logistical problem when they took off on overnight paddling trips: Shoreline campsite options, such as they were, were either bunched too close together or were too far apart for the average paddler. So at the end of the day, there was always the nagging issue of where to sleep.

The Washington Water Trails Association solved this problem by creating four marine trails. After a day of paddling, recreationists using nonmotorized beachable craft can now pull into one of more than 50 campsites and spend the night. While many sites are in parks or private campgrounds, others are independent of the traditional overnight sites and reserved for paddlers. Some pull-ins have access to bed-and-breakfasts and hotels.

Puget Sound paddlers can follow the same trade routes used by Native Americans and early settlers and enjoy the sights that have graced this area for ages: Mount Rainier, Mount Baker, the 8,000-foot peaks of the Olympics, wildlife, and Whidbey Island's sand-and-clay cliffs.

The Cascadia Marine Trail is a 140-mile route from Olympia in south Puget Sound to the Lighthouse Marine Park on Point Roberts, near the Canadian border.

The Willapa Bay Water Trail is a little more challenging in that during low tides, much of the bay is a mud flat. Kayakers can head up the Naselle River or paddle to Long Island for a campsite.

The Lakes-to-Locks Water Trail has approximately 100 access locations and traverses more than 100 miles of shoreline on Washington, Sammamish, and Union Lakes and on the Ship Canal and the Chittenden Locks in Seattle.

The newest marine trail is the Lower Columbia River Water Trail, a 146-mile, two-state trail of tidally influenced rivers from the Bonneville Dam to the Pacific Ocean, mainly on the Columbia River.

Plans are under way for the Northwest Discovery Water Trail, which will link the Clearwater and Snake Rivers in Idaho and Washington and connect the Columbia River to Bonneville.

Marine Trails:

These paddling routes are dotted with campsites reserved for small, non-motorized craft.

47

you know you're in
washington when...
...dogs get their own ski trails

No star shines brighter in Washington's "skinny-ski" firmament than the Methow Valley, located off the eastern slope of the North Cascades. Imagine blue skies, jagged mountain peaks, dry snow, and a groomed trail system that, like the Energizer Bunny, just keeps going and going and going.

By all reports, it's one of the largest and best-maintained Nordic ski areas in the United States and the best in the Northwest. The Methow Valley Sports Trails Association maintains the 124-mile trail system, which is divided into three distinct but connected areas for skiing as well as snowshoeing. There are even dog-friendly trails: Big Valley near Winthrop, Cougar Bait in the Rendezvous area, and Lunatic near Mazama.

It's been Methow Valley's good fortune that Cascade cement—wet, densely packed snow that plagues skiers—rarely falls on the dry side of the mountains. Ocean storms soaked with moisture crawl over the 9,000- to 10,000-foot mountains through rapidly dropping temperatures and dry air. The result is about 7 feet of snowfall a year in the valley, where you might spot the state's largest herd of mule deer.

While western Washington is gray and wet, the Methow Valley boasts sun five days out of seven, enough brilliance that you can soak up the rays on your lodging's deck between outings.

The valley is a four-season destination. It's surrounded by wildernesses, national parks, and Forest Service land. Hundreds of trail miles and countless campsites complement several upscale lodging options.

Peak-sitting Sun Mountain Lodge, the Northwest's oldest and largest cross-country ski resort, is a year-round facility with architecture reminiscent of the traditional rock-and-beam national park lodges. Its pampering amenities include outdoor hot tubs with spectacular views.

Methow Valley:

This outdoor recreation destination is one of the largest and best-maintained Nordic ski areas in the United States.

... hackers become billionaires

In the 1970s William Gates III and Paul Allen were two bright Seattle high school hackers who imagined a wired world in which everyone owned a personal computer and people were connected through a global network.

Microsoft:

Two Seattle high school hackers founded this company, the world's largest software corporation.

Allen later dropped out of Washington State University to become a Honeywell programmer. Gates was living in front of Harvard's computers, resisting Allen's urges to drop out and start a software company with him.

In December 1974 Allen showed Gates a picture of the Altair 8080—the world's first microcomputer kit to rival commercial models—on the cover of *Popular Electronics*. Before they had written one line of code, the pair called Micro Instrumentation and Telemetry Systems (MITS), the maker of the Altair, and said that they had created a software program for it. They were invited to demonstrate the nonexistent program.

Gates concentrated on writing the code; Allen simulated the Altair with a Harvard computer so that the software could be tested. Eight weeks later Allen flew to MITS and entered BASIC on the Altair for the first time. It worked. A few months later BASIC 2.0 was shipped in 4K and 8K versions, incomprehensibly small by today's standards.

Gates dropped out of Harvard, and Microsoft was born. The world's largest soft-

ware corporation has its headquarters in Redmond. Microsoft has been accused of being a "velvet sweatshop," yet it trusts its software developers with key decisions, making millionaires out of many. It has been praised for creating Windows, the most-used operating system in the world, but criticized for its lack of software security.

Allen left Microsoft in 1983 after developing Hodgkin's disease. He built a development company, created Experience Music Project and the Science Fiction Museum (see pages 25 and 75, respectively), and bought the Seattle Seahawks and Portland Trailblazers.

Gates is in the process of giving up day-to-day responsibilities at Microsoft. He will resign as chairman at the end of 2008 to concentrate on the multibillion-dollar Bill and Melinda Gates Foundation.

you know you're in
washington when...
...the pimpled plains remain a mystery

The strange Mima Mounds, rock and dirt piles that are 5 to 8 feet tall and 30 feet in diameter, once sprawled across 20 square miles of the Mima Prairie south of Olympia. Speculation about the origins of the "pimpled plains" has provided much entertainment since explorer Charles Wilkes "discovered" them in 1842.

Home Sweet Home: Hordes of Ice Age pocket gophers migrated to the area behind a retreating glacier. Unable to dig nests in the packed gravel left by the glacier, they spent millennia building mound-shaped nests on top of the ground. There is support for this notion: It's been estimated that 10 gophers on an acre can move 10,000 pounds of dirt and small rocks a year; the mound spacing is similar to underground gopher nests; and cavities filled with silt could be abandoned gopher tunnels.

All Shook Up: Earthquakes created the formations. While building a doghouse in 1980, geologist Andrew Berg hammered a sheet of plywood covered with volcanic ash. The resultant pattern of bumps reminded him of the Mima Mounds. After experimenting he found that his "quakes" shook loose soil into piles, with soft sediments forming mounds.

Green Gardens: Tribal gardeners built mounds on which to grow vegetables.

Mima Mounds:

Origin theories about the large rock-and-dirt mounds range from Ice Age pocket gophers to Paul Bunyan.

Fish Nests: A 19th-century geologist/zoologist theorized that the mounds were fish nests built when the area was underwater.

Frozen Prairie: The prairie thawed after the last Ice Age and fractured into blocks, which melted like ice cubes, eventually changing shape.

Paul Did It: The mythic lumberjack Paul Bunyan and his Irish workers labored to build a wall similar to the Great Wall of China, but the workers eventually quit and left their full wheelbarrows behind. The wheelbarrows rotted, leaving piles of dirt.

Farms and developments have destroyed most of the mounds, but the state has saved 450 acres in the Mima Mounds Natural Area Preserve, complete with viewing platforms, kiosks, and trails.

Back off, fashion police. It's not that we aren't aware of dress-for-success formulas, anorexic runway models, and fashion choices driven by New York and Paris designers. We just don't care.

Washington residents are likely to wear Birkenstocks and fleece jackets, Tevas and shorts with a heavy sweatshirt, backpacks to the symphony, and sunglasses on cloudy days (the sun might come out).

In 2005 Seattle drew the style-savvy hosts of The Learning Channel's *What Not to Wear* show, who couldn't comprehend our waaaaaay too casual style—the hiking boots in the city, the outdoorsy look, the comfort-over-style trend that drives our fashion sensibility.

What they didn't get is the *comfort* factor. While we don't go out of our way *not* to mix and match properly, we don't see the problem with wearing wool socks and Birkenstocks. It's not accurate to describe us as having no fashion sense; just check out the logos on our clothes and backpacks: North Face, REI, Eddie Bauer, etc.

We're experts on dressing as if we were outdoors, where most of us would rather be. We know what *Gore-Tex* and *polypropylene* mean. We understand dressing in layers. Our fashion guru is Seattle's Eddie Bauer, who gave us the first insulated down jacket.

We're not avoiding the latest fashion because we're cheap; we'd rather spend it on a new tent, a high-tech kayak paddle, or Swarovski binoculars. Or a good book, for that matter.

We do admit to having had a fashion moment during the grunge era, but it's not our fault. Musicians wore what they could afford, and in the case of Nirvana's Kurt Cobain, that meant secondhand flannel shirts and ripped jeans.

So back off, fashion police. Other than young people caught up in the latest fad, most of us are confident enough to wear what feels comfortable.

Mixed-Message Fashions:

Washingtonians are known to sport Birkenstocks with wool socks, shorts with fleece jackets, and sunglasses on cloudy days.

It all happened in 1962: *The Jetsons*, the futuristic flip side to *The Flintstones*; John Glenn orbited Earth; the communications satellite was invented; a laser beam was bounced off the moon; and Seattle's answer to urban traffic jams—the monorail—was showcased at the World's Fair.

Although that vision fizzled out, the elevated monorail remains a well-loved icon for visitors and residents despite periodic debates over whether to repair, replace, or retire it.

The demonstration project was built by a German company. After the fair, it was turned over to Century 21 Corporation, which sold it to the City of Seattle a few years later for $600,000. With more than two million riders a year, it is the only self-sufficient publicly owned rail system in the nation.

Today, the elevated trains run in a tube through the Experience Music Project, a rock 'n' roll museum inspired by Seattle native Jimi Hendrix (see page 25). The monorail consists of two cars; each can carry 450 passengers on its 0.9-mile, two-minute ride from the Seattle Center to Westlake Mall downtown.

For all of the forward thinking in 1962, the promise of a wider rail-transit system withered in city councils, although public voters approved of the concept. A recent effort to extend the system was derailed in a series of ill-conceived strategic decisions and major financial problems. But propose demolishing the monorail, and a hue and cry arise. The system always seems to survive another attack, for better or worse.

The monorail occasionally generates unwelcome excitement. A 2004 electrical fire caused a 150-passenger evacuation. A year later, two monorail trains sideswiped each other at a poorly designed spot on the tracks, bringing the system to a halt.

Questions about the monorail's continued use are still being raised, so if you're in town, hop aboard before the future of Seattle's urban transportation becomes history.

Monorail:

This beloved Seattle icon passes *through* a rock 'n' roll museum.

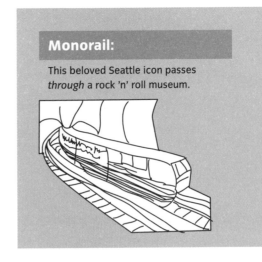

There's something prehistoric looking about dragonflies—with good reason, since they existed millions of years before dinosaurs and had up to 28-inch wingspans. One dragonfly, the common green darner, is the state insect of Washington. It's also called the mosquito hawk or darning needle.

At 3 inches long, the green darner is one of the largest and fastest dragonflies (it can travel up to 35 miles per hour). A male is marked by its green thorax and bright blue abdomen, which resembles a thick darning needle. Its four independently moveable wings have a 4- to 6-inch span.

Males are very aggressive about territory. They patrol about 8 feet off the ground, diving on trespassing dragonflies and devouring mosquitoes and other flying insects. Green darners migrate, but they live only one summer as adults, making a return to their birth pond impossible.

One of the more remarkable things about this dragonfly, says University of Washington zoology professor John Edwards, is its survival mechanism during the one to five years that it spends underwater as a larva, or nymph. Its rectum is a jet-propulsion mechanism, enabling it to dart away from hungry fish by alternately sucking in and then ejecting water.

The nymph has a special extendable lower jaw, called a mask, with which the ferocious

Mosquito Hawk:

The common green darner is the official insect of Washington.

predator seizes its prey, attacking anything smaller than it is (2 inches in the last of several molts). It eventually climbs out of the water looking something like a crumpled plastic bag, then inflates by swallowing air. Once plumped up, the green darner exudes an enzyme that turns its vulnerable body into a hard outer shell in about two hours.

With the biggest compound eyes in the insect world and a nearly 360-degree field of vision, the green darner can detect prey up to 40 feet away. Most of a dragonfly's brain is dedicated to processing what it sees and reacting. And what a reaction! The green darner's speed is complemented by legs that point forward and are covered in spines that form a "basket" to catch prey. And its strong jaws have biting parts than can break insect shells—just like in prehistoric days.

you know you're in
washington when...
... snow keeps falling and falling and falling

Mount Rainier gets all the glory, but Mount Baker has at least two reasons for bragging: the world record for single-season snowfall and the Legendary Banked Slalom.

A gargantuan snowfall in January 1999 helped Mount Baker set the record of 1,140 inches, edging out Rainier's mark by 18 inches. The numbers are even more impressive considering that the record was set at 4,300 feet—1,100 feet below Rainier's measuring station.

Standing 10,788 feet tall, Mount Baker is one of the youngest volcanoes in the Cascades. It has erupted 13 times in recorded history, including once in 1843 when the surrounding forest caught fire. The last eruption was in 1880, although Baker occasionally still lets off steam. Geologists monitor it, predicting that it will erupt again.

In the meantime the volcano is a mecca for snowboarders, in part because it offers a 1,500-foot natural half-pipe. Mount Baker Ski Area was one of the first ski areas in North America to welcome snowboarders, breaking the skiers-only barrier. Now about one-quarter of the snowriders are boarders, and they are among the most loyal patrons.

The ski area is home to the Mount Baker Legendary Banked Slalom, a snowboarding competition that draws elite riders from around the world. The top prize is a golden

Mount Baker:

This dormant volcano is known for its single-season world-record snowfall and an annual snowboarding competition.

duct-tape trophy that one writer has called the Holy Grail of snowboarding.

The event, snowboard's longest-running banked slalom, started in 1985. It was held on Super Bowl Sunday, the slowest day of the year, to minimize conflicts with skiers. Fourteen snowboarders rode the inaugural course; now there are more entries than can be accommodated.

The banked slalom has become such a revered event that a Norwegian snowboarder favored to win a gold medal at the Olympics chose to compete at Mount Baker instead.

To state residents it's simply The Mountain. And on those too-few gloriously clear days, you'll hear them exclaim, "The Mountain is out!"

At 14,411 feet Mount Rainier is the tallest peak in the Northwest and has the most glaciers (26) of any mountain on the U.S. mainland. It's the jewel of Mount Rainier National Park and a draw for two million park visitors a year.

The first American to climb Mount Everest trained on Mount Rainier. About half of 10,000 climbers a year reach the summit, but some die trying.

Captain George Vancouver named Rainier after a British admiral, Peter Rainier, who had fought against the rebels in the Revolutionary War. Native Americans had other monikers for it that translated to "snowy peak," "big mountain," and "place where the waters begin." In the 1930s there was a fierce but unsuccessful effort to rename it Mount Tacoma or Mount Tahoma.

Rainier's last major eruption was about 2,500 years ago; the most recent minor eruptions of steam and ash were in the 1800s. Steep slopes, 35 square miles of ice and snow, nearby major population centers, and the possibility of a huge eruption make Rainier the nation's most dangerous volcano.

Geologists recall the Osceola Mudflow, which took place some 5,000 years ago. About 1,600 vertical feet of Rainier's peak slid away, creating a debris avalanche and mudflow that reached the future sites of Tacoma and south Seattle, the latter approximately 50 miles away.

At least one geologist predicts that if a similar event happened today, Enumclaw, Kent, Auburn, and much of Renton would be destroyed, and the mudflow might reach downtown Seattle.

Most of us would prefer to focus on Mount Rainier's cap cloud, which often hangs like a crown or a halo. The lenticular cloud forms when warm, moist air hits the mountain and then flows upward, where it's cooled by snow and ice and condenses into a cloud.

It's often seen when The Mountain is out.

Mount Rainier:

Washington's signature mountain is also the nation's most dangerous volcano.

Mount St. Helens used to be a picturesque, snow-covered symmetrical peak. But at 8:32 A.M. on May 18, 1980, the southwest Washington volcano erupted, and a postcard-beautiful mountain became a destroyer.

The 250- to 300-mile-per-hour blast and incredibly fast mudflows killed 57 people; destroyed 250 homes, 47 bridges, and 185 miles of roads; and turned about 230 square miles of forest into a lifeless, ash-covered landscape.

Thousands of tiny quakes and minor steam and ash eruptions had long kept geologists interested in St. Helens. Yet everyone was surprised when a 5.1-magnitude earthquake transformed the mountain's upper 1,313 feet and north flank into the largest landslide in recorded history. It was the most deadly and economically devasting eruption ($1.1 billion in timber, agriculture, and infrastructure losses) in the nation's history. Ash, volcanic gas, and steam flew 15 miles high in 15 minutes, and winds blew 520 million tons of ash eastward. Day turned to night in Spokane and Yakima.

The nine-hour eruption sent billions of tons of material down the mountain, some all the way into the Columbia River, blocking the shipping channel.

St. Helens has been the most active volcano in the Cascades over the last 10,000 years. Native Americans have seen an eruption about every 100 to 150 years since A.D. 1400. The Klickitats called it Louwala-Clough, meaning "smoking mountain" or "fire mountain." British explorer George Vancouver named it after a British diplomat, Lord St. Helens.

Today's 110,000-acre Mount St. Helens National Volcanic Monument is a major tourist draw. About one million people a year stop at the Coldwater Ridge Visitor Center inside the blast zone for a view of the mile-wide, horseshoe-shaped crater and the 3,000-foot-wide lava dome.

If the volcano is quiet, visitors are allowed to climb to the crater's edge. For those unable to go in person, a video camera is constantly focused on the mountain; see www.fs.fed.us/gpnf/volcanocams/msh/.

Mount St. Helens:

A 1980 explosion killed 57 people and destroyed more than 1,300 feet of this landmark's symmetrical peak.

you know you're in
washington when...
...an owl is more powerful than a logger

"Save a logger, eat an owl" was the slogan during the 1980s and 1990s, when a verbal, legal, and economic war was waged over the northern spotted owl.

The federal government declared the owls a threatened species in 1990. Restrictions on logging were imposed on hundreds of thousands of acres of public land in Washington to preserve owl habitats, and rules were established to protect old-growth forests and nesting sites, saving an ecosystem.

Since 90 percent of the state's old-growth had already been cut, environmentalists celebrated. But small mill towns were decimated by job loss, grown men cried, and restaurants served spotted owl barbecue.

Up to that point, timber had ruled. In 1900 Frederick Weyerhaeuser signed a $5.4 million deal for 900,000 forested acres in western Washington—at that time, the largest private land transaction in American history. Today, Weyerhaeuser Company has its headquarters in the town of Federal Way.

But as old-growth forests disappeared, so did the spotted owls. Oversimplified, the fight came down to jobs and money vs. environmental issues. Yet blame for the lagging timber economy could not rest solely on the shoulders of owl advocates. That economy started to slide in the 1970s due to corporations shipping logs overseas rather than having them milled at home, computerized

Northern Spotted Owl:

This species was at the center of a major dispute: preserving habitats vs. cutting old-growth forests.

sawmills, and overcutting at unsustainable levels on private land.

Ironically, preserving the habitat may not be enough to save spotted owls, as bullies are moving into their territory. Aggressive barred owls compete for space and food and have killed many of the spotted owls.

A major study reported that spotted owl numbers fell about 7 percent a year in Washington between 1990 and 2005, although the decline was less on federal land with habitat protections. About two out of every three spotted-owl nests noted a decade ago apparently are abandoned, according to researchers.

The 21st-century slogan may turn out to be "Save a spotted owl, eat a barred owl."

What did the nut say to the nutcracker? "You crack me up!" (So much for side-splitting humor.)

The best place in America to admire nutcracker mechanics, art, and creativity is Leavenworth's Nutcracker Museum (www.nutcrackermuseum.com), the only such museum in the nation.

Tchaikovsky's *Nutcracker* ballet was introduced to the United States in 1944 and inspired an interest in toylike nutcrackers. American collectors began their trade in earnest in the 1950s, many starting with the nutcrackers brought home by U.S. soldiers who were in Germany during World War II.

Arlene Wagner (aka the Nutcracker Lady)—a former ballet dancer and producer of *The Nutcracker*—first bought nutcrackers in the 1960s. She and her husband, George, couldn't stop collecting. In 1995 they started the Leavenworth museum in self-defense. They now have one of the world's largest collections, with more than 5,000 nutcrackers on display.

About 1,000 of the museum's nutcrackers are stars in Arlene's 188-page coffee-table book, *The Art and Character of Nutcrackers*. It shows the breadth of construction styles and materials, often capturing the cultural milieu behind each nutcracker's form.

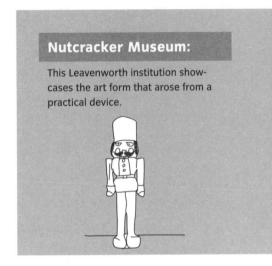

Nutcracker Museum:

This Leavenworth institution showcases the art form that arose from a practical device.

Cracking nuts dates back tens of thousands of years, as evidenced by nuts and tools found in an Israeli bog. Nutcrackers moved from purely utilitarian objects to works of art by the 15th century. The Leavenworth museum has examples of early, ornate versions as well as modern ones.

Visit the museum yourself to see an ancient Roman nutcracker, nut cutters from Asia, silver nutcrackers that matched Victorian table settings, a Napoleon screw nutcracker from France, and a praying monk nutcracker from Italy.

Today, the stereotypical nutcracker is that sword-toting, white-bearded, uniformed man usually seen at Christmas, but it is only a small splinter of the nutcracker world.

you know you're in
washington when...
... the "Angels of Mercy" is overhead

Olympia, not Seattle, is Washington's capital.

Lushootseed-speaking tribes lived in the area for thousands of years before an 1830s trading post was built near the future site of Olympia. Traders and trappers were followed by Catholic missionaries and settlers along the northern leg of the Old Oregon Trail.

Olympia was originally called Smithfield by Levi Smith, who staked one of the earliest claims to the land, when it was still part of the Oregon Territory. In 1848 Smith fell out of a canoe and drowned; Edmond Sylvester inherited his claim and promptly renamed the town Olympia, after the nearby Olympic Mountains.

When the new Washington Territory's governor arrived in 1853, he declared Olympia the capital. Construction of the modern Legislative Building, the last domed capitol built in the United States, was completed in 1928. It took five years for Scottish artistans to carve the Mount Rainier sandstone and Italian artisans to carve the marble used in construction. The carvings include stone ox skulls, honoring the state's ox-cart pioneers.

The capitol dome is one of the tallest self-supporting, all-masonry domes in the world. Three major earthquakes caused the dome to shift and crack. After the third quake, a 6.8-magnitude event in 2001, with the epicenter just 15 miles away, the 90,000-pound dome was permanently fastened to the building.

None of the three quakes ruined the five-ton "Angels of Mercy" chandelier, a masterpiece by Louis Comfort Tiffany. It hangs from a 101-foot chain in the center of the 174-foot-high dome. The chandelier, the largest produced by New York's Tiffany Studios, arrived in Olympia aboard a train.

The capitol also has the world's largest collection of bronze that bears the Tiffany mark.

Olympia:

This south Puget Sound city is the capital of Washington state.

you know you're in
washington when...
...the state's wildest ride is on four feet

Seldom does a horse race create such strong opinions—but that's what happens when horses die.

The World-Famous Omak Suicide Race started as a 1935 publicity stunt for the Omak Stampede, an annual rodeo in northeast Washington. Billed as "the wildest ride in Washington," it's also called the world's most dangerous horse race because at least 20 horses have died since 1983; three horses died in 2004 alone.

Four races are held the second weekend of August. The first three start at night, when riders, almost all Native Americans, gallop their horses toward the edge of sandy Suicide Hill, which is as steep as a staircase. About 200 feet below is the cold Okanogan River.

The near-blind descent is thrilling, but it's also a recipe for collisions, falls, broken bones, and horse fatalities. Falling riders and mounts cartwheel into and step on each other as too many horses are funneled into a narrow swath at the river's edge. The horses then must cross the 150-foot-wide Okanogan River, scramble uphill, and dash for the finish line.

To riders from a poverty-stricken reservation, a $15,000 pot can make the Suicide Race pretty attractive. Some say that it preserves a cultural tradition, but that argument wins few converts in light of the injuries to and deaths of equine participants.

In 2005 a newspaper reporter wrote that security guards tried to stop people from taking photographs of injured riders and horses. Floodlights were turned off, leaving medics and injured riders in near-dark conditions but shielding them from observing spectators.

Apparently there are some aspects to the World-Famous Omak Suicide Race that organizers would just as soon not share with the rest of the world.

Omak Suicide Race:

Horses plunge down steep Suicide Hill and across a river during this controversial rodeo race.

Dozens of lob-tailing, spy-hopping, flipper-slapping orcas are the stars of Washington's waters. Often called killer whales, orcas are the largest members of the oceanic dolphin family.

The federal government has given the southern resident population endangered species status. People from around the world visit the San Juan Islands for a gas-guzzling boat ride among these animals, which depend on unpolluted waters.

The 1977 movie *Orca: The Killer Whale* reinforced the myth of their danger to humans. (Fortunately, it wasn't a popular movie.) Although the official state marine mammal doesn't attack humans, orcas are the most effective predator in the ocean, able to kill fish, seals, seabirds, sharks, turtles, and whales. Orcas may eat an average of 500 pounds a day to power their 27- to 33-foot lengths and four to six tons through the water.

Resident pods in Washington State waters are known for their family values. A family unit is the matriline, a single female and her descendants; her daughters' sons and daughters are part of the line. Females can live 80 or 90 years, so a pod of whales might have three to five generations traveling together.

Transients, residents (most commonly seen in the San Juans), and ocean pods are the

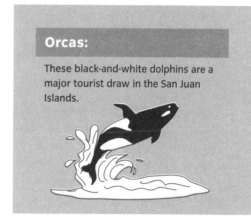

Orcas:

These black-and-white dolphins are a major tourist draw in the San Juan Islands.

three main orca groups. Residents tend to be more vocal than transients, even though they live in the same water. Resident pods have dialects specific to that pod.

Orcas have signature black-and-white markings, stocky bodies, and large dorsal fins. Color patterns and nicks and scrapes on the fins allow researchers to identify (and name) each orca.

In the 1980s orcas underwent reputation rehabilitation. People began to object to the killer-whale label and to orcas being confined to tanks and doing tricks in Sea World–type settings. The 1993 film *Free Willy* addressed this issue. Keiko, the orca that played the title role, later was returned to his original Nordic waters, but he kept returning to shore, probably looking for human interaction. Never able to integrate into ocean life, Keiko died in 2003.

It's an open-and-shut case. Thanks to Willapa Bay, where about 17 percent of the oysters consumed in the United States are harvested, South Bend claims bragging rights as the Oyster Capital of the World.

Long before white settlers made money shipping the bivalves to cities, Native Americans worked the tide flats. Once the newcomers connected their taste buds to their wallets, the town of Oysterville became a center for harvesting and shipping. Although it is now a shadow of its former self, a few varieties are still harvested from commercial beds there.

Western oysters, renamed Olympia oysters when the state capital was selected, were once plentiful. But overharvesting and pulp mill pollution almost wiped them out. Now most of the oysters on Washington's public beaches are Pacific oysters, introduced from Japan. Other types include Eastern and European flat oysters.

While Olympias are small, Pacific oysters have a deep cup. The latter have been grown in Washington since the early 1900s. Varieties are often named after their cultivation sites, such as Hama Hama, Quilcene, and Snow Creek.

To those with sensitive taste buds, West Coast and East Coast oysters have distinct flavors and textures because of differences

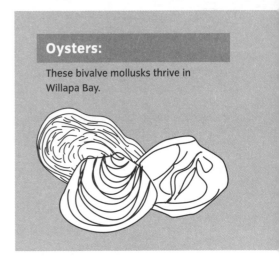

Oysters:

These bivalve mollusks thrive in Willapa Bay.

in salinity, water flow, and species. Some aficionados swear that they can even taste the difference between Willapa Bay, Penn Cove, and Chuckanut oysters, varieties grown in three Puget Sound bays.

An oyster's two-part shell is hinged together and can open and shut with amazing speed. It can't be pried open by hand because of a powerful adductor muscle, so harvesters must stick a tough, sharp oyster knife inside and cut the muscle. This skill is called shucking, which can lead to slurping raw oysters off the half-shell.

Don't worry about swallowing a pearl. Although an occasional one turns up, they're tiny.

No need to walk 2,650 miles to get a sense of the crown jewel of America's trail system, the Pacific Crest Trail (PCT). Just pick up the PCT at the Bridge of the Gods on the Columbia River and head north through the Cascades.

It's only about 500 miles to Monument 78 on the Canadian border. Along the way you'll see dramatic mountain peaks (Mount St. Helens, Mount Adams, Mount Rainier, Glacier Peak, and Mount Baker among them) and wildlife, including mountain goats, black bears, and cougars. Add to that canyons, glaciers, snowfields, alpine lakes, and wildflower-covered meadows.

Of course there are also logging roads, clear-cuts, railroad grades, and an occasional highway. In the fall you'll be more apt to notice spots of color, including crimson huckleberry bushes and the yellow needles of the Western larch. The trail crosses several wildernesses and national forests. While you might see dogs and horses, you won't see bikes or motorized vehicles.

The PCT in Washington began as the Cascade Crest Trail in the 1930s but eventually became part of the Mexico-to-Canada system. Some of the original markers can still be seen.

In some sections the hiking is easy; in others it takes backcountry skills and stamina, not to mention food-laden packs because there are no fast-food joints or even many towns along the way. Although you start less than 200 feet above sea level at the Columbia Gorge, you'll hike many miles above the 6,000-foot mark.

While most hikers take the PCT one section at a time, many people spotted in September are "through hikers"—those that started at the Mexican border and are making one last push to reach the Canadian border before the sometimes-fickle weather dumps snow in the high country.

Pacific Crest Trail:

Five hundred miles of this 2,650-mile trail system run from the Columbia River to the Canadian border.

The Cascade Mountains divide Washington State, one-third to the heavily populated west and two-thirds to the sparsely populated east. This geographical split created a corresponding philosophical divide that recently showed up in the state legislature.

Republican lawmakers, complaining that outnumbered eastern Washington politicians and constituents suffered from the rules made by western Washington legislators (mostly Democrats), proposed a bill to split the state into two states. It was the latest sally in the usually mild-mannered culture wars, fueled by a full tank of stereotypes with some geographical-driven realities.

It's said that westerners are members of the Sierra and roadside service clubs; easterners are NRA members and tote jumper cables and chains. West of the Cascades, a culinary outing is going to an ethnic restaurant; east of the Cascades, it's homegrown steaks on the backyard grill. The West has major-league sports teams, green landscapes, Puget Sound, and rain; the East has minor-league baseball, scablands, Lake Chelan, and irrigation. The West has urban gridlock for up to three hours a day; only tractors cause traffic jams in the East.

Stereotypes continue: Western Washington residents are upscale, liberal, college educated, not very religious, and addicted to espresso. They listen to rock 'n' roll and world music (plus the Dixie Chicks), are light on family values, and have flexible standards. Eastern Washington residents are blue collar, conservative, light on higher education, and religious. They drink black coffee, play country music (except for the Dixie Chicks), and emphasize family values.

The West features urban centers and high-tech companies; the East has small towns and farms. Western Washington supports environmental protection, zoning laws, gun restrictions; eastern Washington supports property rights and gun rights.

The East supports tax cuts, even though it accepts more tax money per capita than it generates. The rest comes from those wine-sipping heathen hippies west of the Cascades. Ironically, much of the wine they drink comes from eastern Washington grapes.

Philosophical Divide:

Stereotypes separate western Washington (urban, upscale, liberal) from eastern Washington (rural, blue collar, conservative).

you know you're in
washington when...
...a pig becomes a pawn

Washington isn't a top pig-raising state, but it has an interesting swine story. We like our Pig War on San Juan Island so much that there's an annual reenactment, even though a porker was the only casualty.

In 1846 America and Great Britain were in a snit over who would win the claim to the San Juan Islands. You see, the exact location of the international boundary between Canada and the United States hadn't been nailed down.

Eight years later, the question remained when U.S. Customs officials landed on San Juan to collect duties on a British sheep farm. An arrest warrant was issued, claiming that the officials had trespassed on British soil. In 1855 a U.S. sheriff and his men grabbed 35 sheep from the Hudson's Bay Company to pay for back taxes, a move that didn't go over well with the British.

Meanwhile, a few Americans had settled on the island. In June 1859 a farmer named Lyman Cutlar shot a Hudson's Bay Company pig that was rooting after his potatoes. Tempers flared, and the British threatened to arrest Cutlar.

Matters weren't helped when a hot-headed U.S. brigadier general got involved. After hearing various complaints from American settlers, the general ordered Captain George Pickett to occupy the island, which

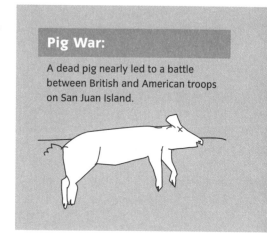

Pig War:

A dead pig nearly led to a battle between British and American troops on San Juan Island.

he did with 66 troops on June 27, 1859. Royal Marines then landed from a British warship. After much arguing and posturing, U.S. reinforcements were sent; the Brits responded with five warships and more than 2,000 men.

Three months after the porcine fatality, President James Buchanan heard about the Pig War and essentially told everyone to chill. A joint occupation was negotiated, and in April 1860 British troops established a camp at the opposite end of the island from U.S. troops. Today, visitors to San Juan Island National Historical Park can still visit American Camp and English Camp.

Kaiser Wilhelm I of Germany eventually arbitrated the boundary; his decision made the San Juan Islands U.S. land in 1872.

When it comes to farmers' markets, high-tech Seattle is lovingly low-tech at the oldest continuously operating and historically authentic market in the United States.

We can thank onion prices for Pike Place Market. In 1906–07 the cost of onions in Seattle increased tenfold. Rather than cry about it, Seattle residents and the city council cut out the middleman and created a public street market with a meet-the-producer philosophy that still exists.

When the market opened on August 17, 1907, 10,000 shoppers swamped eight farmers selling produce from their wagons.

The market developed character over the years with a signature neon sign and giant clock, a stew of classes and races, and communists and evangelists on soapboxes. But a bad 1941 fire; empty stalls during World War II, when Japanese-Americans (many of them growers and market sellers) were forcibly relocated to internment camps; and the development of chain grocery stores depressed the market.

By the 1960s fewer than 100 farmers were left at Pike Place Market. It faced relocation or demolition several times, with plans presented under the cover of kill-it-to-save-it or simply to eradicate it as an obstacle to progress. One failed idea was to replace the market with a giant parking garage. A

Pike Place Market:

Founded in 1907, it is the oldest continuously operating and historically authentic farmers' market in the nation.

1971 public vote led to the creation of the historic district and protected Pike Place Market for the foreseeable future.

Today, about nine million visitors shop and eat at the market, now home to about 190 commercial businesses, 50 restaurants, 200 day stalls, and about 300 apartments, most reserved for low-income elderly residents.

Visitors marvel at the fishmongers throwing (and catching) fish, wander through the subterranean warren of eclectic shops, admire the colorful flowers and produce, take home artists' creations for gifts, and enjoy the views of the Olympic Mountains.

If the Space Needle is Seattle's signature landmark, Pike Place Market is its soul.

you know you're in
washington when...
...there are rain shadows and convergence zones

Despite its wet reputation, most of Washington State isn't all that moist. Seattle, for instance, ranks 44th among U.S. cities in average yearly rainfall at 36.2 inches. Mobile, Alabama, and New York City both collect more rain (65 and 39 inches, respectively).

And yet, Perry Como's wistful thinking aside, it's doubtful that the bluest skies you've ever seen are in Seattle. The city has 226 cloudy days a year because the rain arrives in spits and showers. A Houston thunderstorm might drop an inch in a half hour; in Seattle it could drizzle all day just to hit the quarter-inch mark.

Ironically, more sunglasses per capita are bought in Seattle than in any other major city. After six months of almost nonstop dreary skies, a sunny day is like a spotlight shining in your eyes. Here, shades and smiles go together. (No wonder the happy face was invented in Seattle.)

Most of the trees that earn Washington State its Evergreen State nickname are on the west side of the Cascades. The closer to the Pacific Ocean, the larger they grow, thanks to 132 to 144 inches of rain a year in the Hoh Rainforest in Olympic National Park.

But most of that rain never reaches Puget Sound because the Olympic Mountains block the storms and create a rain shadow.

On the northeast corner of the Olympic Peninsula, Sequim's average annual rainfall is 17 inches, giving the so-called Banana Belt the honor of being the driest Pacific Coast climate north of Los Angeles.

Storms split around the Olympics and reconverge over Puget Sound to create the infamous convergence zone just north of Seattle, where weird weather often means thunderstorms or hail when nearby areas are clear.

Dry weather rules east of the Cascade Mountains, which block most of what's left of the moisture from the Pacific. Ellensburg in central Washington averages 10 inches per year; Spokane in eastern Washington averages 17.

The bluest skies you've ever seen are in . . . Yakima?

Rain Shadow:

The Olympic Mountains block most Pacific Ocean storms, resulting in modest rain fall for Seattle and other Puget Sound cities.

you know you're in
washington when...
...pink elephants aren't a hallucination

Some of the things we hold dear were created before homogenization steamrolled diversification, including roadside attractions that would have a hard time gaining traction in the 21st century.

Take pink elephants. In 1951 Archie Anderson and his two brothers, owners of Elephant Car Wash in Seattle, set a rotating pink elephant over their business. The landmark at Denny and Battery Streets has 380 blinking bulbs and 70 pieces of neon.

Bob's World Famous Java Jive in Tacoma was built in 1927. This coffee-pot-shaped club, 25 feet high and 30 feet in diameter, once was home to two monkeys: Java and Jive.

If tea's more your thing, go to the red-and-white Teapot Dome Gas Station in Zillah—the oldest operating gas station in the nation until it stopped pumping in 2003. Its shape originally was intended to mock President Harding's Teapot Dome scandal.

Hat 'n' Boots gas station, built in 1955 near Georgetown, featured a 44-foot-diameter cowboy hat and 22-foot-tall boots. It even had a patent. Restoration is underway.

Seattle's Ye Olde Curiosity Shop started in 1899 on the waterfront. John Wayne, Charlie Chapin, Katharine Hepburn, and Teddy Roosevelt all browsed there, perhaps attracted by the shrunken heads from South America or the Lord's Prayer

inscribed on a grain of salt. Ironically, many Northwest Native American and Eskimo objects that have passed through the shop are now on display in major museums in three countries.

A similar shop is Marsh's Free Museum in Long Beach, home to Jake the Alligator Man. Some claim to have seen Jake in a Texas carnival.

Seattle's Lusty Lady is one attraction that could gain traction in any century. The peep-show biz is located across from the Seattle Art Museum. Known for its creative marquee messages, Lusty Lady plays off the museum's exhibits (advertising "Chuck Clothes" in reference to artist Chuck Close, for example). Even museum director Mimi Gates has called the marquee a Seattle landmark.

Roadside Attractions:

From giant elephants and cowboy boots to peep-show marquees, Washington has its fair share of roadside oddities.

WORLD FAMOUS BOB'S JAVA JIVE

Elk were hunted to the brink of extinction in Washington. In 1913 a handful of Rocky Mountain elk from Yellowstone National Park area were introduced to the South Cascades near Yakima to rebuild the population. Each winter, smart elk migrated to the lowlands and chose items for their winter nibbles from ranchers' haystacks and orchards.

An occasional elk was acceptable; herds that had multiplied exponentially and ate their way through landowners' assets were not. By 1939, when the state established the Oak Creek Wildlife Area, there were 3,000 elk and a lot of irate ranchers and farmers.

An 8-foot-high fence nearly 100 miles long (from south of Yakima to near Ellensburg) was built in the mid-1940s, stopping the herds from drifting into the lower elevations to forage. That protected human assets but reduced winter acreage for the elk. Starving elk didn't make hunters happy, so the state started feeding elk during the winter.

The plan worked. The herds survived, the hunters were happy, and the elk kept breeding and multiplying. Now there are about 10,000 elk scattered in various herds in the area. During severe winters, up to 7,000 elk visit feeding stations, looking for several pounds of hay per day per elk.

Rocky Mountain Elk:

Washington State feeds the Yakima herds every winter to keep them out of orchards and farms.

Visitors go to the Oak Creek feeding station to watch 1,500 elk or more gather for the daily dispensation of hay, mostly done by volunteers who also run the interpretive center and give tours. It's as close as most visitors will ever come to an elk, although the gathering is more like a cattle call than a scene from the wild.

For those who also want to see bighorn sheep, a feeding station is located at the Cleman Mountain site in the Oak Creek Wildlife Area. A small herd of bighorn from British Columbia were introduced into the area in 1967; now there are about 200 animals.

Ah, the law of unintended consequences.

Seattle's professional sports teams have produced more unusual roof stories than league championships.

The SuperSonics played in the only National Basketball Association game stopped for rain. Rain dripping through the Coliseum (now KeyArena) roof formed a puddle at half-court before the Sonics played the Phoenix Suns on January 5, 1986.

After a short delay for a good mopping, the game began—but drips turned into a steady flow, and a ball boy couldn't keep the floor dry. A minute into the second quarter, with the Suns up by 11 points, the game was postponed.

Workers were able to patch the Coliseum roof fairly quickly; the Seattle Mariners were not so lucky. On July 19, 1994, four acoustic tiles fell into Kingdome seats before a contest between the Mariners and the Baltimore Orioles. With no quick fix available, the Mariners had to spend the last 22 days of the strike-shortened season on the road, and their National Football League counterparts, the Seattle Seahawks, had to play the first three home games of their season at the University of Washington's Husky Stadium.

It was the beginning of the end for the building that everyone loved to hate. About a year after the Mariners' new baseball sta-

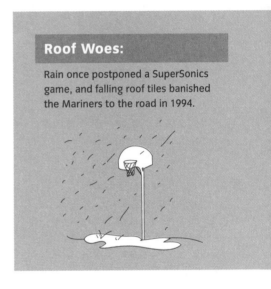

Roof Woes:

Rain once postponed a SuperSonics game, and falling roof tiles banished the Mariners to the road in 1994.

dium, Safeco Field, was built, the Kingdome was imploded in 2000. Now two new stadiums have their own roof stories.

Safeco Field has a 22-million-pound retractable roof that covers 8.9 acres (about 54,000 umbrellas could cover the same area). More than half of Mariner fans travel more than an hour to see a game, and the team doesn't want them to stay home because of a threat-of-rain forecast.

Qwest Field has a permanent roof that covers about 70 percent of the stands. Despite the fact that games are played during the rainy season, of all the home football games since 2002, only a few have been played in the rain.

What's more unusual than the world's largest rosary collection is where it is permanently displayed: in the Columbia Gorge Interpretive Center in Stevenson, not far from the Columbia River.

A rosary is a string of beads used in devotional prayers, most commonly by Catholics. But Native Americans, Buddhists, Jews in pre-Christian times, and others also have counted beads in a spiritual framework.

Don Brown, who lived most of his life in North Bonneville, collected 4,000 rosaries from around the world. His interest was piqued when, in a hospital as a child, he saw rosaries worn by the Sisters of Mercy.

Brown became a Dominican brother and collected rosaries for about 60 years. As word of his collection spread, rosaries arrived from around the world. Donors included President John F. Kennedy, who gave Brown the wooden-bead rosary he carried during World War II.

Conductor Lawrence Welk, Notre Dame football coach Lou Holtz, and Boys Town founder Father Flanagan also contributed. Some rosaries in the collection were blessed by popes, including the first one blessed by Pope Pius XII after his election.

The rosaries are made from wood, gems, bone, ivory, seashells, olive pits, and even bullets. The oldest ones in the collection were made in the 18th century in Spain and Bavaria.

Brown donated the collection to the Skamania County Historical Society, which he founded. There wasn't much display space in the little museum, so the rosaries were hung from hundreds of bird-cage hangers. Eventually they were moved to special display cases in the Columbia Gorge Interpretive Center as part of the Spiritual Quest exhibit.

Each rosary has been catalogued by its donor, origin, material, and a place, person, or event associated with it.

Brown died in a car accident in 1975. He was buried with the rosary that he had in his pocket.

Rosaries:

The world's largest collection of rosaries, a string of beads used in counting prayers, is located in Stevenson.

If humans had to work this hard to procreate, the world's population might not be in the billions.

Washington's iconic salmon return from the sea to their home streams through a gauntlet of fishing hooks, nets, orcas, sea lions, and harbor seals. The survivors swim up creeks and rivers, working against the current with manic perseverance to their places of birth.

There they spawn and often undergo a physical metamorphosis that distorts their bodies. Most species then die, their carcasses providing food for eagles and other wildlife.

Washington's salmon species are Chinook, coho, chum, sockeye, and pink. Chum develop large, canine-looking "teeth" when they spawn, giving rise to the nickname dog salmon. Pinks are also called humpies because males get a large hump on their backs during spawning.

Pinks live only two years, so they don't put on much weight. Chinook can live up to nine years, plenty of time to amass poundage. Though they usually weigh 10 to 50 pounds, a few Chinook reach 100 pounds or more.

The fry of some species leave home immediately, heading to the ocean or Puget Sound. Coho lay eggs in the fall, but their fry don't emerge until the following spring and don't leave for the sea for another full year. Sockeye, the most flavorful salmon, require a lake to rear their fry for a year or two.

Wild stocks of salmon have been declining for more than a century in Washington. Almost 200 wild stocks are of special concern or are at risk of extinction. In the long term, habitat loss is more dangerous than hooks and sea lions.

The Wild Salmon Hall of Fame, sponsored by the Pacific Northwest Salmon Center (PNWSC) in Belfair, celebrates those who protect salmon and salmon habitats. The PNWSC also plans to establish a Salmon Center on Hood Canal for education and research.

Salmon:

Washington's iconic fish return to their places of birth to spawn.

you know you're in
washington when...
...gunkholing the archipelago can take years

On land we look at a mountain and see a peak. On water we see a peak and call it an island. In the American San Juans in Washington, 172 islands are the tops of drowned mountains, sitting at the junction of the Strait of Juan de Fuca and the Strait of Georgia.

The San Juan Archipelago (the American San Juans, plus the Gulf Islands of British Columbia) might number 450 or 700 or some other figure, depending on who's counting and the definition of island. Many "islands" appear only at low tide.

Most of the American San Juans are between western Washington and Vancouver Island in British Columbia. San Juan Island is the largest. Four others are served by the Washington State ferry system: Orcas, San Juan, Lopez, and Shaw.

The archipelago is a favorite destination for boaters practicing gunkholing, the art of leisurely cruising and anchoring in coves for a quiet overnight stay. Most of the islands are undeveloped and can be reached only by a kayak or private boat; several are marine state parks. And most are in the rain shadow of the Olympics, so the weather is drier than much of western Washington.

The islands' names recall early explorers. The Spanish reached the area in 1790, led by Francisco Eliza, who named the group of

San Juan Archipelago:

These islands are located at the junction of the Strait of Juan de Fuca and the Strait of Georgia.

islands after the viceroy of New Spain (Mexico), Don Juan Vincente de Guemes Pacheco de Padilla Horcasitees y Aguayo, Conde Revilla de Gigedo. Eliza polished the apple a bit, ergo San Juan Island, Guemes Island, and Padilla Bay. Other Spanish names survived in shortened versions.

Some Spanish monikers disappeared when the British renamed many of the islands. Then Americans named everything not already identified on British charts, usually after naval officers.

In 1847 the British Admiralty reworked the charts to eliminate confusion; the officers ignored many of the American names, saved the British ones, and revived or relocated many of the Spanish ones.

you know you're in
washington when...
... it's illegal to kill a hoax

State residents take their Sasquatch, aka Bigfoot, very seriously. The majority of U.S. sightings of the elusive hairy creature come from Washington.

Depending on your tall-tale preferences, Sasquatch is between 8 and 11 feet tall and weighs 700 to 2,000 pounds. In Skamania County it's against the law to kill the beast; violators face a $1,000 fine and five years in jail. It may be the only U.S. county in which Sasquatch is a protected species.

The Web site of the Washington State Sasquatch Search Group shows pictures of (alleged) Sasquatch footprints and an (alleged) Sasquatch behind a tree at Wedik-end Creek in Grays Harbor County. Foot-print molds and photographs like these haven't convinced many that Sasquatch—or multiple Sasquatches—are hiding out in Washington's hills.

The legend spread nationwide when Sasquatch became a fictional character in Marvel Comics' universe, first appearing in *Uncanny X-Men #120* in April 1979. Several American Indian legends include an earlier version of Sasquatch, which shows that sitting around the fire and telling stories is a time-honored tradition.

Humans in ape suits and cleverly created "footprints" account for much of the supposed proof of Sasquatch's existence. The

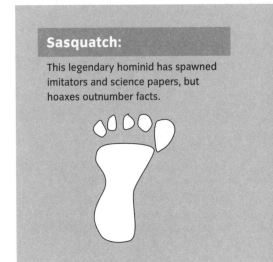

Sasquatch:

This legendary hominid has spawned imitators and science papers, but hoaxes outnumber facts.

1967 classic grainy film footage of the legend was exposed as a hoax in 2003 by the person who created it. He told a reporter, "It's time to let this thing go."

But Washington persists with a variety of tributes. The state is home to Squatch, the Seattle SuperSonics team mascot since 1985; Sasquatch Books, which published *Field Guide to the Sasquatch;* the Sasquatch Reading Award; the North Cascades Sasquatch Loop, an eight-day biking adventure; and the Sasquatch! music festival at Gorge Amphitheater.

Warp drives, time machines, phasers, tricorders, robots, androids, lightsabers, Klingon daggers, the Alien Queen, and Captain Kirk's command chair are all at home in Washington.

Paul Allen, cofounder of Microsoft, turned two of his passions, rock 'n' roll and science fiction, into two Seattle museums: the Experience Music Project (see page 25) and its companion, the Science Fiction Museum and Hall of Fame.

The modern science fiction genre started with the original sci-fi magazine, first published in 1926, and the sci-fi movies of the silent-film era. The genre went from brass-bra babes to bug-eyed monsters before writers reached for the philosophical.

Now science fiction authors use the genre to explore the present as well as the future, making aliens a reflection of our own dreams, fears, and prejudices. To that end, the Science Fiction Museum demonstrates how sci-fi reflects the human condition, promotes critical thinking, and invites us to ponder the universe's infinite possibilities.

Allen gave his personal sci-fi collectibles a $20 million, 13,000-square-foot home, then went in search of more donations and loans with his sister, cofounder Jody Patton. Their exhibits contain a fascinating mish-mash of fiction and fact: A 1951 Dick Tracey radio, a life-size model of the Alien Queen from the 1986 movie *Aliens,* and a half-size replica of the rover *Sojourner* used in 1997 on Mars are all part of the museum collection.

Visitors can enjoy the museum's intergalactic saloon (think *Star Wars*), study a science and science fiction timeline, and listen to a recording of Orson Welles's 1938 *War of the Worlds* radio broadcast, which convinced many that there was a Martian invasion in New Jersey.

Sci-fi pulp magazines; props from *Planet of the Apes* and *Blade Runner;* and a complete first-edition, signed set of Isaac Asimov's Foundation trilogy are held in trust for the future.

Enter the museum and you can almost hear, "May the force be with you."

Science Fiction Museum:

This Seattle institution pays homage to alien invasions and space explorations.

75

you know you're in
washington when...
...you're kidnapped by terrifying pirates

Seattle's laid-back reputation is shattered every summer by things that go fast.

During Seafair, a monthlong outdoor party, high-speed hydroplanes churn a section of Lake Washington into rooster tails and the Blue Angels amaze crowds with aeronautical acrobatics. While spectators bask in the frivolity and speed, many residents leave town, unable to stand the whine of the hydros and the roar of jets.

The city and hydroplanes have been dance partners since 1950, Seafair's inaugural year. That June a Seattle-built hydroplane named *Slo-mo-shun IV* shattered the world speed record on water by averaging 160.32 miles per hour on two Lake Washington runs. Stan S. Sayres Memorial Park is named for the pilot, although it is more often called Sayres Pits, especially during Seafair.

The fascination with speed extended to the Blue Angels, now a longtime fixture at Seafair. And in 1955 Alvin "Tex" Johnston, flying 400 feet above Lake Washington at more than 400 miles per hour, did a pair of barrel rolls in a Dash-80 prototype, the forerunner of the Boeing 707.

There has always been more to Seafair than its loudest events, however. The Milk Carton Derby arrived in 1972 when competitors built watercraft using empty milk cartons as flotation devices, then raced them on Green Lake. And the Torchlight Parade has become one of the nation's largest nighttime parades, with crowds of 300,000 and a television audience of about a half million viewers.

The Seattle Seafair Pirates likewise provide entertainment. When this public-service troupe isn't visiting hospitals to cheer up sick children, it builds on its bawdy, swashbuckling reputation by performing raids, "kidnapping" folks, and participating in various Seafair events.

Seafair:

Seattle's biggest party draws hydroplanes, stunt pilots, and pirates.

you know you're in
washington when...
...saltwater, sea stars, and sand rule

Having a choice can be a delightful experience. Strawberry, cookies-and-cream, or vanilla? Hawaii, Bermuda, or Mazatlan? Or in the case of Washington's shorelines, Cape Flattery or Cape Disappointment? San Juan Island or Point No Point?

Let your fingers slide along the map from Semiahmoo Spit near Blaine and the Canadian border down the east Puget Sound coastline to the mouth of the Nisqually River; north to Port Townsend; west along the Strait of Juan de Fuca to Cape Flattery; and south along the Pacific Coast to Cape Disappointment.

Puget Sound—a glacier-carved valley flooded by ocean water when an ice dam broke some 13,000 years ago—has 500 square miles of water, hundreds of islands, and 1,400 shoreline miles. It's part of the Salish Sea, the traditional name for the inland marine waters from Turnwater to Johnson Strait in British Columbia, used by the Coast Salish tribes.

There are many places to fling your beach towel and dash to a tide pool, but saltwater is only part of the story.

The 1,232-mile-long Columbia River creates much of the state's southern boundary after flowing south from the Canadian border. Several dozen other rivers and hundreds of lakes offer beachgoers myriad water's-edge adventures.

Shoreline:

From Semiahmoo Spit to Cape Disappointment, Washington has shorelines of every variety.

Washington has the largest natural sand hook in the nation (Dungeness Spit); the Northwest's deepest harbor (Port Angeles); and the northwesternmost point in the continental United States (Cape Flattery), with incredible views of Tatoosh Island, sea stacks, marine life, and caves.

Much of the shoreline beauty and ecosystem value has been damaged or destroyed, but a large-scale estuarine project to restore and protect hundreds of miles of Puget Sound shoreline is under way.

There's more at stake than beach parties. Puget Sound is home to 18 threatened or endangered species, and half rely on shoreline habitat for food and shelter. Pacific salmon, for instance, return to Puget Sound's rivers and creeks to spawn.

The challenge is to provide for the least glamorous critters as well as humans looking for a spot on the beach.

Down-and-out people often live on Skid Row, a squalid place of quiet desperation. The original phrase was Skid *Road*. It probably originated in the 1850s in Seattle, although Vancouver, British Columbia, also claims the honor.

Loggers built wood skids and sometimes greased them to decrease friction, hence the phrase "grease the skids." The parallel planks were used as a ramp to skid logs from the top of Yesler Way, named after the owner of the area's first steam-powered sawmill, down to the waterfront. (Skids were used in Northwest logging camps, too; some historians believe that the associated terminology started there.)

Many of the poorest workers built the barest of shelters along Skid Road. In Seattle the road separated downtown from an area of brothels, bars, and flophouses to the south. Eventually, that area became known as Skid *Row,* whose population usually consisted of alcoholic transients "on the skids."

In 1897, when gold was discovered in Alaska, Seattle became a major supply stop. Miners not only bought goods in the Skid Road district before going north by ship but also created more business for dance halls, brothels, and saloons.

The phrase "Skid Row" slowly spread across the country and came to mean a

Skid Road:

This phrase probably originated in 1850s Seattle, where loggers used wood skids to transport lumber to the waterfront.

road (or row) to nowhere, with no association with logging.

The Depression took whatever hope might have been left in Seattle's Skid Row, and the name became synonymous with down-and-out folks in a bad part of town. The film and musical *Little Shop of Horrors* spread the phrase even wider with the song "Skid Row (Downtown)" in 1960.

After a certain amount of gentrification, the Seattle Skid Row area became the Pioneer Square–Skid Road Historic District. Many homeless still call this area home.

They drift like snowflakes, large white birds with black wingtips dropping out of the turbulent shades-of-gray sky, feathers brilliant in breakthrough sunlight as they glide in groups to land in the Skagit Valley.

While older humans head south each winter to escape the wet winters of western Washington, snow geese arrive from their breeding grounds in Siberia, usually a nonstop 3,000-mile, 48-hour flight.

Snow geese winter in large numbers in Washington, also home to the greatest concentration of wintering bald eagles on the U.S. mainland and a fair number of trumpeter swans.

But only snow geese can blanket a field, not seeming to mind living wing-to-wing in huge flocks. Families frequently stay together (couples mate for life, but if one dies, the other will mate again) part of the winter; they chatter—constantly—to keep together family groups. It's almost deafening when there are 10,000 geese in one field.

The 500-acre Fir Island Farm/Hayton Farm Goose Reserve near Conway, part of the 13,000-acre Skagit Wildlife Area, is a prime target, thanks to farmers who plant winter wheat as a cover crop for the geese in cooperation with the state Department of Fish and Wildlife.

Snow geese movements are, in part, driven by tides and light. They roost on bays and feed in mudflats at low tide.

Some bird-watchers try to get closer to take pictures of the huge flocks and spook them into taking off. This makes for a spectacular sight, but it stresses the birds at a time when they're consuming calories for the trek north in a few months.

It's against the law to disturb, harass, or haze migratory waterfowl. If they're flushed in a panic, they may fly into power lines, be shot by hunters, or be taken by eagles. That's no way to treat a snowbird.

Snow Geese:

Flocks of these large geese fly 3,000 miles from Siberia to their wintering grounds in the Skagit Valley.

you know you're in
washington when...
...courthouse records are worth stealing

You think 21st-century politics are rough? Try stealing a courthouse in the late 1800s.

Pacific County residents still like to tell the story. Oysterville, on the Long Beach Peninsula, had been the county seat since 1855. By the 1880s the native oysters were almost gone, and Oysterville's economy had collapsed.

Across Willapa Bay, South Bend was booming; the Northern Pacific Railroad ended in the town promoted as the Baltimore of the Pacific. In 1892 voters approved moving the county seat to South Bend. Oysterville residents charged that the ballot box had been stuffed by railroad workers.

The most reliable accounts of what happened next came from eyewitnesses, including county commissioner J. A. Morehead. On February 5, 1893, 85 men boarded two steamers at South Bend. One steamer pulled into Oysterville and the other into Sealand, where about 50 of the raiders were greeted by a man armed with a shotgun.

Jim Morrison agreed to let them come ashore only if they had a round of drinks with him. After fulfilling their obligation, the raiders joined their friends at the courthouse, where a muscled tailor-taxidermist kicked in the door.

The county auditor arrived and lost his temper, expressing his displeasure by using a chair leg against numerous heads before

order was restored. The mob left with some records and furniture. Here the phrase "unmitigated gall" is useful. A bill was sent to the county commissioners for services rendered during the looting of the property. It went unpaid.

Not many years later, South Bend's faltering economy put it at risk of losing the county seat to Raymond. Residents immediately pledged $10,000 to help build a new courthouse. The commissioners agreed, but the contract was mysteriously lost, and the county had to pay the whole bill.

In 1911 South Bend had its courthouse. A 29-foot rotunda crowned by stained glass made it one of the grandest among county courthouses. Locals called it the Gilded Palace of Extravagance.

South Bend:

In 1893 South Bend residents crossed Willapa Bay and "liberated" courthouse records from Oysterville.

you know you're in
washington when...
... you visit the Wheedle's house

Sketches on a coffeehouse placemat led to Seattle's 605-foot signature structure, the Space Needle, built for the futuristically themed 1962 World's Fair. Architect John Graham transformed the sketches into a space-age totem, a flying saucer atop a wasp-waisted tripod with curved legs.

After King County refused to fund the project, five private investors saved the day, buying a 120-foot-square plot at the Seattle Center in the nick of time. During the largest continuous concrete pour in the West, 467 cement trucks poured 5,820 tons of concrete into a hole 30 feet deep in about 12 hours to anchor the structure.

In keeping with the fair's "Century 21" theme, the Needle was painted Astronaut White, Orbital Olive, Re-Entry Red, and Galaxy Gold. It was the tallest building in the West (eclipsing Smith Tower, the record-holder since 1914), yet built to withstand earthquakes and winds of 200 miles per hour.

At the 500-foot level, the Eye of the Needle became the world's second revolving restaurant. The Eye and a second restaurant later closed so that a larger restaurant could be built. It rotates every 60 minutes via a 1.5-horsepower motor. Observation deck views include the Seattle skyline, the Olympic and Cascade Mountains, Mount Rainier, and Puget Sound.

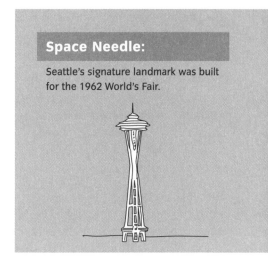

Space Needle:

Seattle's signature landmark was built for the 1962 World's Fair.

The Needle fell over in a 1989 April Fool's joke by a local television station; emergency lines were swamped, and the station later apologized. But it wasn't the first "fall." In 1962 Maggie and Mike Moloso recorded "Wasn't It a Mighty Day When the Needle Hit the Ground." It became a regional hit, but World's Fair organizers were not amused. Abruptly, radio stations stopped playing the song.

The Space Needle has starred in movies, including *It Happened at the World's Fair* with Elvis Presley, and in the television sitcom *Frasier*. In the 1974 children's book *Wheedle on the Needle,* author Stephen Cosgrove introduced a furry creature called Wheedle who lives on top of the Space Needle and causes its lights to flash.

It was the smile seen 'round the nation, an improbable end to a season, a moment that may have saved baseball in Seattle.

The 1995 Mariners, perennial underdogs, were 13 games back in mid-August when a "refuse to lose" attitude, late-inning comebacks, and an improbable Angels' losing streak led to a season-ending division tie. Seattle won the one-game playoff.

With a 2–2 American League division series with the Yankees on the line, an 11th-inning double by Edgar Martinez sent Ken Griffey Jr. sliding across home plate with the game-winning run. There was Griffey, grinning under a pile of Mariners while pandemonium broke out in the Kingdome at the team's first playoff series win.

Until that fall it looked as if the Mariners might leave Seattle, but renewed interest eventually led to a new stadium. In 2001 the team won 116 games; it has struggled since.

Unfortunately, Washington sports fans suffer from a paucity of modern-day professional championships. There are three on the books: The Seattle Sounders, a United Soccer Leagues First Division team, won a title in 2005; the Seattle Storm won the WNBA title in 2004; and the Seattle Super-Sonics won the NBA title in 1979.

The Seattle Seahawks busted out of the

Sports:

Many Seattle-based sports teams have had memorable moments, but a college football rivalry stirs up the most passion these days.

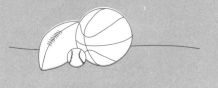

football futility box with their first Super Bowl game in 2006 but lost.

Prior to the Sonics title, the biggest ticker-tape sports parade in Seattle may have been for 19-year-old Helene Madison, who brought home three Olympic gold medals in 1932. Few can remember that the Seattle Metropolitans became the first U.S. team to win hockey's Stanley Cup when they beat the Montreal Canadiens—in 1917.

The most fiercely fought rivalry these days pits the University of Washington Huskies football team (co–national champs in 1991) against its cross-state rival, the Washington State University Cougars. It's a classic west vs. east, urban vs. rural competition with copious amounts of trash-talking. An Apple Cup win can salvage even a terrible season.

you know you're in
washington when...
... you hear that the state song is "Louie Louie"

How did "Louie Louie," variously described as one of the dumbest songs ever written and the missing link between 1950s rock 'n' roll and 1960s hard rock, become a candidate for the state song?

Washington's official state song, Helen Davis's "Washington, My Home," was adopted in 1959, displacing the unofficial state song, "Washington Beloved." The latter's lyrics were written by historian Edmond Meany with music by Reginald de Koven, who wrote "O Promise Me" and other operettas.

Not impressed with Davis's lyrics, some residents started a semiserious movement in the 1980s to dethrone "Washington, My Home." Their pick? "Louie Louie." Excluding Paul McCartney's "Yesterday," no other pop or rock song has been recorded more.

OK, so Richard Berry's 1955 calypso–style ballad is about a lovesick sailor in a bar pining for his woman—but it does have a Washington state tie. A Tacoma band, The Wailers, added a few twists and made it a regional rock 'n' roll favorite, although their version did not hit the national charts.

The Kingsmen had better luck, turning the party song into a hit (number two on the Billboard Hot 100 chart) in 1963. Their version was basically undecipherable, the first step in becoming a legend. Parents and politicians alleged that the lyrics were obscene (rumor had it that the smutty words could be understood if you played the 45-rpm single at a slower speed). The FBI tried to prove it was obscene but gave up after two and a half years.

Eventually, fans lobbied for state-song status. A 1985 legislative resolution said that the state needed a "contemporary theme song that can be use to engender a sense of pride and community"—not to mention tourism and economic development.

The state Senate actually approved the resolution, but the House did not.

State Song:

"Washington, My Home" had to hold off a challenge from "Louie Louie."

STATE SONG

Louie, Louie oh no

~~Washington, my home~~
Wherever I may roam
This is my land, my
    native land,
Washington my home

you know you're in
washington when...
... you don't need the initials D.C.

Forty-one states were admitted to the nation before one was finally named after a president. Ironically, Mount Rainier, named long before Washington State, honored a British soldier who fought against General George Washington's troops.

About six million people live in the "Other Washington," more commonly referred to as the Evergreen State. That's another irony since most of the state is arid, not evergreen. Had history played out differently, the state could have had a British or Spanish name—or no statelike name at all, had the Native Americans successfully resisted the white invasion.

The federal government created the Oregon Territory in 1848. Settlers north of the Columbia River petitioned Congress to carve out the Columbia Territory, real estate from the river to the 49th Parallel. Congress obliged but called it Washington.

Since then, residents and the legislature have been dreaming up items to receive State This or State That status, reaching far beyond the traditional motto and song.

One state song wasn't enough. There's also a state *folk* song, Woody Guthrie's "Roll On, Columbia, Roll On." If you're singing, you might as well twirl to the state dance, the quadrille, a square dance of French origin, while wearing the state tartan of red, white, blue, yellow, black, and green.

The container ship *President Washington* is the state's official ship. The steelhead trout is the state fish; the orca earned its niche in 2005 as the state marine mammal.

The state flower, the coastal rhododendron, was voted on in 1892 by women who couldn't vote in political elections. The western hemlock is the state tree, the apple is the state fruit, and native bluebunch wheatgrass is the state grass.

The American goldfinch won the state bird votes of schoolchildren and the Washington Federation of Women's Clubs. Sharing airspace is the state insect, the carnivorous green darner dragonfly. Leaving no stone unturned, the legislature also approved a state gem and a state fossil: petrified wood and the Columbian mammoth, respectively.

State Symbols:

Like other states, Washington has a host of official symbols, but it is the only state named after a president.

When you want to get away, *really* get away, Stehekin is the clear winner. It's the most remote community in Washington, so far away that you can reach it only by float-plane, a slow-going scenic boat ride with the Lake Chelan Boat Company, or a multi-day hike through the Cascade Mountains. It's the only nonisland town in the state that can't be reached by car.

Located at the edge of the Stehekin Valley, Stehekin ("ste-HEE-kin") is wedged between the headwaters of the 55-mile-long fjordlike Lake Chelan and the 8,000-foot peaks of the North Cascades. At nearly 1,500 feet deep, Chelan is the third-deepest lake in the United States.

Stehekin is the jumping-off point for back-country exploration of the 62,000-acre Lake Chelan National Recreation Area and the North Cascades National Park.

The town is home to one calling-card phone booth, a road that runs a few miles up the valley for vehicles that have been barged in (some are 50 years old), a one-room schoolhouse, 312-foot Rainbow Falls, the Stehekin Pastry Company, a post office, some accommodations, an information center, and a restaurant. Sorry, no television service.

The journey to this community of about 100 permanent residents is half the fun. Visitors enjoy the ride on usually calm

Stehekin:

The most remote town in Washington is accessible only by boat, floatplane, and hiking trail.

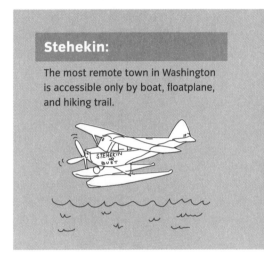

waters as the lake, rarely wider than 2 miles, squeezes into the mountains. A float-plane is quicker, and you have the option of returning on a boat. During the summer boats can bring a few hundred people a day to Stehekin, although most visitors stay for only a few hours.

Stehekin's Native American name roughly translates to "the way through." For centuries the route upriver to Cascade Pass was a trading route; later it was adopted by prospectors and then hikers. The community started in the 1880s with gold and silver prospectors. Since they never hit the mother lode, there was never a need to punch a road through the mountains. Their failure left Stehekin to nature, a handful of appreciative residents, and visitors looking for peace and quiet.

you know you're in
washington when...
... you encounter Stonehenge

Visitors to the original Stonehenge near Salisbury, England, aren't allowed close enough to hug the ancient stones. But in Maryhill, visitors on a high, windy bluff above the Columbia River can have an up-close-and-personal visit with Stonehenge—or at least a full-size, nearly identical replica of it.

Road-builder extraordinaire Sam Hill bought 6,000 acres overlooking the Columbia in 1907 to establish a Quaker farming community. Only a few Quakers showed up, and the small community (named Maryhill, after his daughter) was later destroyed by fire, leaving only Stonehenge standing.

When Hill built Stonehenge, he mistakenly believed that the original was a sacrificial site, so his version was a memorial to all soldiers still being sacrificed to wars. It may have been the first monument in the United States to honor World War I dead. The altar stone was dedicated in 1918 and the project completed in 1930, shortly before Hill died.

Hill was known for more than Stonehenge. In 1913 he built the first paved road in Washington, the 3.6-mile Loops Road near Stonehenge. In 1907 he created the first chair of highway engineering in the nation, at the University of Washington.

His own home, a poured-concrete, castlelike edifice overlooking the Columbia Gorge, was also named Maryhill. Before the project was completed, Loie Fuller, a pioneer of

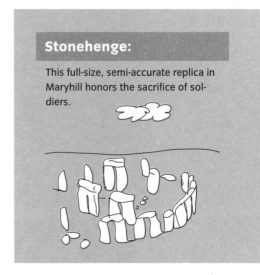

Stonehenge:

This full-size, semi-accurate replica in Maryhill honors the sacrifice of soldiers.

modern dance and an inventor of theatrical lighting techniques, proposed turning the mansion into an art museum. Hill agreed.

Fuller used her Parisian connections to buy a large collection of Auguste Rodin sculptures, perhaps the finest in the country, for the museum. Queen Marie of Rumania helped dedicate the unfinished Maryhill Museum of Art in 1926. Thousands attended the ceremony. The museum includes gifts from Queen Marie, a room of Russian icons, and a large collection of Hill's road-building memorabilia.

In the end, financially devastated by the Depression, the eccentric Hill asked to be left alone. His tomb is at the base of the Stonehenge bluff.

you know you're in
washington when...
... you're standing on the northwest edge

Captain James Cook was poking around the Northwest in 1778, trying to find an elusive passage back to the Atlantic Ocean that would earn him a huge reward. According to the logs, he discovered a cape that "flattered us with the hopes of finding a harbour."

There was no harbor, but a name was born —Cape Flattery, today the northwestern-most point of the continental United States.

That same year, Captain James Meares visited a small island a half mile off Cape Flattery. He reportedly named it after Tatoosh, the chief of the Makahs, a tribe that used the island as a summer camp for whale-hunting and fishing.

In 1850 a surveyor for lighthouse sites chose what he called Tatoochi Island as one location. The federal government bought the island in 1855, but workers received a cold reception. Smallpox had killed hundreds of Makahs two years earlier, so they were not enthusiastic about white neighbors.

Lightkeeper turnover was high because of poor pay, harsh winters, and isolation. In 1885 keepers with families started being assigned so that the lighthouse would be "no longer at the mercy of the rollicking bachelors who have had possession since its establishment," according to one report.

Perhaps it was the gunfight that clinched this change. Two keepers went outside and fired at each other, apparently missing and calling it a draw. It turned out that another keeper had removed the bullets from the shells before the duel.

Eventually the families "civilized" the island, starting a tiny school and bringing in a piano and a cow. A weather station was added, and in 1977 the lighthouse was automated.

The Makah Tribe recently renovated the mainland's Cape Flattery Trail, turning a muddy, dangerous path at the edge of high cliffs into a cedar boardwalk and a maintained packed-earth, 0.75-mile trail. The reward is a spectacular view of ocean waves pounding the rocky cliffs, nearby Tatoosh Island, and if sightseers are lucky, sea otters, orcas, puffins, and/or harbor seals.

Tatoosh Island:

An 1857 lighthouse stands on this former Makah Indian fishing and whaling camp off the northwesternmost edge of the U.S. mainland.

you know you're in
washington when...
...your tongue twists pronouncing state names

Native American languages are the source of many Washington town names: Humptulips, Hamma Hamma, Walla Walla. Puyallup, Palouse, Pysht. Dosewallips, Duckabush. Skokomish, Skagit, Stillaguamish, Sequim, Skykomish, Snoqualmie, Spokane, Seattle.

Some of them are easy to pronounce only because they're the settlers' interpretation of the original, both in spelling and sound, or a derivative from the Chinook ("shin-NOOK") jargon. This shorthand language—a mixture of Spanish, French, English, and Indian words—was used by nearly 100 tribes as well as traders and pioneers.

Visitors are surprised at the local pronunciation of some names that don't appear to be in the tongue-twisting category. They'll pronounce Spokane, which was named for an eastern Washington tribe, "spo-KANE" instead of "spo-KAN," meaning "children of the sun" or "sun people."

Sequim is another seemingly easy two-syllable word, except it's not. The correct pronunciation is "squim." Sekiu is pronounced "SEE-cue," Shi Shi is "shy-shy," and Pysht sounds something like "pished."

In Washington you "do the Puyallup," meaning that you attend the Puyallup State Fair. Be sure to pronounce it "PEW-al-up," not "POO-yal-lup." The word means "generous people," an indication of the tribe's reputation for dealing with traders.

Most visitors (and many state residents) don't come close to succeeding on their first attempts at Pend Oreille ("PON-dohr-AY").

To confuse matters, not everyone familiar with Washington State place names pronounces them the same. Locals occasionally use their own version, even if the rest of the state evolves a different pronunciation. For instance, some would argue that Yakima should be pronounced "YAK-i-MAW" (think Wichita), not "YAK-i-muh."

Over the decades local pronunciations may fade away as new residents fail to pick up on the hometown nuances and television becomes a linguistic leveler. After all, if a newscaster says "YAK-i-MAW," what newcomer would argue?

Tongue Twisters:

To the uninitiated, Washington State place names can be notoriously hard to pronounce.

WELCOME TO PUYALLUP! THAT'S PEW-ol-up.

88

Ancient forests have driven some tree-huggers to great lengths, prompting them to compete for bragging rights to finding the largest tree of a species.

In northwest Washington those trees can take on mythic proportions, causing grown men to hike for 30 miles to measure a tree, armed with expensive survey lasers and a calculator. Stand in awe of a towering and impossibly broad conifer, and it's easy to catch the fever.

The largest old-growth trees and the largest temperate rainforests on the U.S. mainland are in three ocean-facing river valleys on the Olympic Peninsula. Hoh, the largest temperate rainforest in the world, is joined by Queets and Quinault.

A combination of 145 inches of rain a year, mild winters, summer clouds, and fog produce temperate rainforests populated by long-lived giants. A Douglas fir can grow several feet a year and live up to 800 years; a red cedar can live longer than 1,000 years.

The biggest trees in the state are on the Olympic Peninsula—the western red cedar, Sitka spruce, coast Douglas fir, Alaska cedar, western hemlock, and Pacific silver fir. Some are the largest living trees of their species.

Giants reach more than 300 feet with bark that is more than a foot thick. A few in

Trees:

The Olympic Peninsula is home to three temperate rainforests and many big trees.

Olympic National Park stand out: a western red cedar that is 61 feet in circumference and 178 feet tall, making it the world's largest (and possibly oldest) specimen of its species; a Douglas fir that measures 44 feet and 5 inches in circumference; and a Sitka spruce that stretches 305 feet tall.

Ancient forests are more than ancient trees. A complex, highly evolved, cooperative ecosystem—from fungus to fallen trees to Roosevelt elk and woodpeckers—exists in and under a multilayered forest canopy. An old-growth forest is also home to more than 1,200 plants and 300 animal species.

Temperate rainforests don't have exotic flowers or humidity, but their biomass exceeds that of tropical rainforests. In some places 500 tons of living matter exist per acre.

Although no one has tulip fever like the Dutch, visitors to the Skagit Valley bring a good case of it with them as they wander about brilliantly colored tulip fields during April's Tulip Festival.

They can thank the Dutch and a virus. By the 17th century, the Dutch had turned tulip-raising into an art form. How ironic that the cause of the spectacular feathers and flames of the most in-demand tulips was a mutation-causing virus that eventually weakened and killed the bulbs.

The more infected the plant, the more beautiful the flowers—and the higher the price in the speculation economics of Tulipomania in the 1630s. Even after the tulip bubble burst, Holland's growers slowly spread their influence around the world, eventually reaching the Skagit Valley.

When the U.S. government banned bulb imports for 20 years in 1926, Holland growers sent members of their families to America to build bulb farms. Today, no one is trading gold and oxen for a single tulip bulb, but passion for the beauty of tulips has survived in the Skagit Valley.

The Tulip Festival is a monthlong event that includes art, antiques, alpacas, gardening tours, fireworks, and the Tulip Pedal, in which bicyclists wind through the fields. The festival's extended time frame spreads

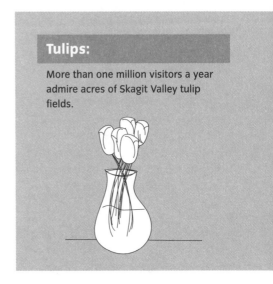

Tulips:

More than one million visitors a year admire acres of Skagit Valley tulip fields.

out the one million people who attend each year and makes it more likely that the tulips will be at their peak sometime during the event.

The Skagit Valley, now one of the world's major producers of iris, tulip, and daffodil bulbs, is subject to the same pressures that every agricultural area faces, including growth at the expense of farmland. Once numerous, there are only two major tulip growers left: the Roozen family, owners of Washington Bulb Co., and the DeGoede family, owners of Skagit Valley Bulb Farm and Tulip Town.

you know you're in
washington when...
...UFOs are part of the culture

A chain of nine peculiar-looking aircraft was sighted by pilot Kenneth Arnold in crystal-clear skies as he searched for a downed plane near Mount Rainier on June 24, 1947.

They reflected sunlight and caught his attention. Arnold was upset because, despite his familiarity with aircraft, he couldn't identify them as they quickly flew from Mount Rainier south to Mount Adams.

Arnold reported what he saw. Many did not believe him, though his pilot friends were less skeptical. His account made headlines around the world, and other sightings of similarly described objects were reported in the next few days.

Arnold's report is considered the first UFO sighting in modern history, and his description of the objects "flying like a saucer" morphed into the phrase "flying saucers."

According to a 2005 poll by the University of Connecticut, 60 percent of Americans believe that life exists on other planets, and 70 percent think that it is likely those life-forms can travel through space.

A large percentage of those folks must live here. The state ranks seventh for unidentified flying object sightings according to the *U* Database, a 20-year compilation of data by a UFO researcher.

The director of the nonprofit National UFO Reporting Center is Peter B. Davenport, who lives on a former intercontinental ballistic missile site in eastern Washington. The alien-hunter and investigator claims to have seen UFOs, including several in Washington. He's hard to dismiss out of hand with his degrees in Russian, biology, genetics, and the biochemistry of fish and his MBA in finance and international business. Even nonbelievers respect Davenport's sound approach to investigations.

The center has a Web site (www.nuforc.org) and a hotline for reporting unidentified flying objects, although it gets more crank calls than legitimate reports.

Washington State also has its own chapter of the Mutual UFO Network; and, although it doesn't report unidentified flying objects, the Washington State Ghost Society likewise deals with visuals that are hard to prove.

UFOs:

Pilot Kenneth Arnold made what is considered the first modern UFO sighting near Mount Rainier in 1947.

you know you're in
washington when...
...you're looking up at the sidewalk

Today's exploding toilets usually result from student pranks, but in late-19th-century Seattle, they were a natural phenomenon.

Seattle was built on a tidal plain. It was best to drop your pants at low tide because at high tide the downtown area often flooded, ergo sewage in the streets and the exploding-toilet syndrome. All that changed after the Great Fire of 1889, which led to a plan to rebuild downtown at a higher level.

Business owners couldn't wait for the wheels of bureaucracy to turn. They rebuilt their stores at the original level. When the city finally raised the streets, front entrances were as much as 36 feet below street level in the new 33-block Seattle Underground.

Going from one store to another (or one tavern to another) across the street often required climbing and descending ladders. Newspapers reported that more than a dozen inebriated men died after falling. Regardless, merchants continued to open the underground floors, using glass cubes set into the above-their-heads sidewalks for illumination.

But rats began to take control underground. In 1907 the city closed the underground after three residents died of bubonic plague. Bounties were given for each rat tail brought in, though some clever entrepreneurs started breeding rats for the reward.

Now the dusty, spooky (some *Night Stalker* scenes were shot there), abandoned subterranean area can be visited on Bill Speidel's Underground Tour. The tour starts in a restored 1890s saloon, drops into three underground sections, and meanders through Pioneer Square. The underground is not for the claustrophobic or those with spiked heels.

The viewable area is only a few blocks long, but the guides' semislapstick patter makes it worth the price of admission. Visitors can catch up on Seattle's embarrassing secrets, humorous stories, and colorful (and often corrupt) founding fathers.

But no exploding toilets.

Underground:

Subterranean passages pass by the first-floor storefronts of old Seattle, created when the city raised the streets.

SEATTLE STOREFRONTS

you know you're in
washington when...
... you fest with the best

The 1970s saw difficult economic times, particularly in western Washington. Boeing went bust, and the timber industry slid downhill—fast. But Seattle refused to let reality interfere with a good party.

Founding fathers and mothers birthed two music events, Northwest Folklife (Memorial weekend) and Bumbershoot (Labor Day weekend), and turned them into two of the largest and longest-running urban music festivals in the United States.

The two operate on different energies: Folklife starts summer; Bumbershoot ends it. Folklife is free; Bumbershoot charges admission. While Folklife gives local and regional artists a chance to shine, Bumbershoot edges into crowded rock-festival territory.

Folklife is the place to connect with your roots. The festival, which started as a project of the Seattle Folklore Society, is a sampling of arts and culture that thrives thanks to 6,000 local and regional folk artists and 1,200 volunteers.

Its major draw is music, but it also offers dance, film, storytelling, crafts, workshops, and food and can draw 250,000 people. Each year a cultural focus is selected; in 2006 it was the Arab communities of the Northwest.

Urban Festivals:

Seattle parties for days with the Northwest Folklife Festival and Bumbershoot.

Bumbershoot (a slang term for umbrella) was free for its first 10 years, before a decision to bring in national and world acts necessitated admission charges. In addition to concerts, spectators can enjoy flat-track roller-derby races, admire rock posters, laugh at comedians, watch films, and explore technology-based art.

Four other Seattle festivals are worth noting: Earshot Jazz Festival, the city's most important annual jazz event; the three-week-long Seattle International Film Festival, which may be the largest independent film festival in the nation; Hempfest, one of the world's largest marijuana law–reform gatherings; and Seafair (see page 76).

Come rub elbows with explorers Meriwether Lewis and William Clark in Long Beach. Their statues stand along the town's main drag, sharing the salty air with fun-seeking tourists.

Lewis and Clark led the U.S. Corps of Volunteers for Northwest Discovery on an exploration of the uncharted West, reaching the conjunction of the Columbia River and Pacific Ocean in November 1805. "Great joy in camp," Clark wrote in his journal when they arrived. It was probably the last joy they experienced while in the future state of Washington.

The last month of the trip was supposed to have been an easy paddle using the westward currents of the Columbia to reach the ocean. Instead, the explorers fought life-threatening rapids as well as high winds in the Columbia Gorge, the same type of winds that today thrill windsurfers.

Food was often cold, because trees (firewood) along the river were almost nonexistent. Waterfowl provided meat, but the flocks' noise kept the exploration party awake. Every day's paddle brought more irritations. While the Native Americans were generally friendly, the fleas were not. The explorers were trapped by fierce storms. Journals reported that they were continually wet and that their leather clothes rotted. Once they landed near the ocean, they searched

Voyage of Discovery:

Lewis and Clark ended their expedition where the Columbia River meets the Pacific Ocean.

for days for a decent campsite for the winter but found none.

The Clatsop Indians told the explorers that there were elk herds on the south side of the Columbia, in what is now Oregon. They paddled across the river and set up camp and stayed until spring, although the weather was just as miserable.

Today, the Lewis and Clark Interpretive Center, perched on the 200-foot-high cliffs of Cape Disappointment State Park honors their journey.

The expedition leaders' statues look toward the Pacific, but you can almost sense the undercurrent of their thoughts after 4,162 miles, 18 months of exploration, and heavy doses of physical misery. Perhaps, "Can we go home now?"

With all due respect to the Vidalia onions of Georgia, there's nothing like a Walla Walla Sweet. And you won't cry a river while cutting them.

They're fresher, sweeter, and milder than typical late-summer and fall-harvested storage onions. Fresher because they're delivered to market without months in a warehouse. Sweeter because they have 6–15 percent sugar content (compared to 3–5 percent in typical storage onions). And milder because they have less sulfur content and contain less than 5 percent pyruvic acid. It's the acid in the sulfur that causes tears, although the sulfur allows for longer storage.

About 40 growers produce 39 million pounds of the jumbo-size round onions in the Walla Walla Valley of southeast Washington (and a token slice of northeast Oregon).

The variety was a Johnny-come-lately as onions go. Native Americans used wild onions; Pilgrims brought onions on the Mayflower and ate them at the first Thanksgiving dinner. It wasn't until the late 1800s that the ancestors of today's sweet onions were planted in the Walla Walla Valley.

A French soldier, Peter Pieri, brought sweet onion seeds from the Island of Corsica. Pieri and his Italian immigrant neighbors invested in more seeds and started an onion-growing tradition in the valley, but Giovanni Arbini is generally credited with the development of the early Walla Walla.

In 1923 he discovered that some of his crop matured in late June, weeks ahead of the rest. A couple of years of using seeds from those early maturing onions created a premium sweet onion that would eventually be recognized as the Walla Walla.

Now harvested from mid-June through August, the crop is celebrated each July during the Walla Walla Sweet Onion Festival.

To get the most out of your bag of short-storage Walla Walla sweets, recycle a pair of clean panty hose. Drop in an onion, tie a knot, and repeat the process for as many onions as you have. Hang the hose in a dry location, cutting below the lowest knot to retrieve a sweetie.

Walla Walla Sweets:

These onions are famous for their size and sweetness.

you know you're in
washington when...
...maples and hollies reign

A calm oasis in a city infamous for its traffic snarls is but a baseball throw away from vehicular frustration. Washington Park Arboretum, a few miles from downtown Seattle, is a local favorite and the official state arboretum.

Puget Mill Company logged hundreds of acres for about 60 years before 1920. When the timber work was done, 300 acres were turned into the Broadmoor Golf Club and 230 acres were given to Seattle, which developed a park/arboretum with the University of Washington.

In 1936 the Seattle Garden Club donated $3,000 to hire the Olmstead Brothers landscape company (designers of New York's Central Park) to design the first plantings. The plant collections were laid out in the traditional manner, from the simplest to the most advanced families of trees.

During the Depression the Works Progress Administration paid about 500 men to work on the park. They built many features that still stand today, including Azalea Way and the Stone Cottage.

Washington Park Arboretum has North America's largest collection of *Sorbus* (known as mountain ash in the United States), oak, and maple and the second-largest collection of species hollies.

Wander the grounds, and you'll find collections of conifers and camellias, crabapples and cedar, magnolia and Japanese maples. Keep an eye out for 139 plants on the endangered species list; 4,600 plant varieties from around the world; and the state flower, of course—the coast rhododendron.

Several nice touches make the arboretum stand out from others in the public-collection field, including a waterfront trail over two small islands in Seattle's largest wetland and the nearby Museum of History and Industry.

There's also a visitors center and an authentic three-and-a-half-acre Japanese garden designed by Iida Juki in 1960; it features a teahouse, a pagoda, and a 200-year-old Kobe lantern.

Washington Park Arboretum:

This 230-acre oasis includes North America's largest collection of oaks, maples, and mountain ash.

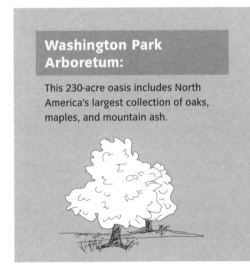

you know you're in
washington when...
... a massacre helped create the Oregon Territory

The Whitman Massacre at Waiilatpu near the Columbia River is one of the most infamous episodes in pioneer settlement. Fourteen missionaries and settlers were killed by Indians on November 29, 1847, starting the Cayuse War and shocking Congress into creating the Oregon Territory in 1848.

Dr. Marcus Whitman, a Presbyterian elder, and his wife, Narcissa, one of the first two white women in Oregon Country, established the mission in 1836 in the Walla Walla Valley. Few were converted, but the mission became an important rest stop for emigrants. In 1843 Whitman led the first large group of wagon trains and about 1,000 pioneers from Fort Hall, Idaho, establishing the Oregon Trail as a viable route.

Two years later, as tensions between Native Americans and pioneers increased, the Nez Perce warned that the Cayuse and Walla Walla tribes were going to attack a wagon train. Whitman rode out with the warning. After much posturing on both sides, the Indians backed off.

The situation deteriorated when pioneers brought measles in 1847. Dozens of Cayuse died despite efforts by Dr. Whitman to save them. The decimated Cayuse suspected that they were being poisoned. Their customs dictated that if an important tribal member died while being treated by a medicine man, then the healer had to die.

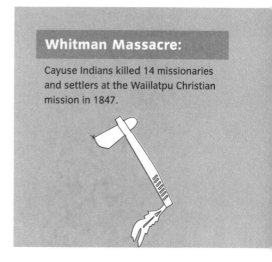

Whitman Massacre:

Cayuse Indians killed 14 missionaries and settlers at the Waiilatpu Christian mission in 1847.

Two Cayuse killed Whitman, murdered 13 others at Waiilatpu, and took hostages. The Hudson's Bay Company paid a ransom of 126 blankets and shirts, 600 rounds of ammunition, 12 flints, and seven pounds of tobacco for the hostages.

The story reached Congress in May 1848, where debates over whether the proposed Oregon Territory should be slave-free dragged on. Hearing the news, Congress created the Oregon Territory on August 13, 1848 (without slaves).

The Cayuse eventually turned over five tribesmen. A four-day trial brought a guilty verdict, although witnesses were not at the massacre. The men were hanged on June 3, 1850; the rest of the Cayuse were sent to a reservation.

you know you're in
washington when...
... a wagon train rolls through town

If ever there was an unlikely town to have ties with authors, it would be Winthrop. This community in north-central Washington was isolated until 1972, when State Route 20 opened through Washington Pass in the North Cascades.

Native Americans lived in the area for 9,000 years. Trappers showed up in the 1800s, followed by gold-seeking miners, homesteaders, and Harvard graduate Guy Waring, who founded Winthrop in 1891 at the confluence of the Methow and Chewuch Rivers.

The town was named after Theodore Winthrop, a 19th-century Yale graduate and author.

Except for the original log town hall, Waring owned every building on the main street. Waring, who hated liquor, opened his Duck Brand Saloon to keep out the worst taverns but tossed out the most inebriated.

Despite his finger-in-every-pie approach to business, Waring went bankrupt in 1916 and returned to the East Coast, leaving behind his showpiece log cabin, which locals had dubbed The Castle. His stepson lived in it before the Episcopal Church bought it. In 1943 it was purchased and preserved as the main building of the Shafer Historical Museum.

Another author with ties to Winthrop helped build the foundation that would lock

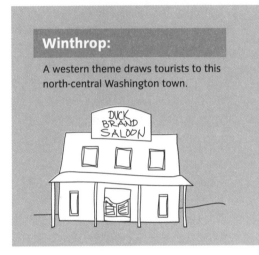

Winthrop:

A western theme draws tourists to this north-central Washington town.

the town into its history. Owen Wister, Waring's Harvard roommate, drew ideas for America's first western novel, *The Virginian*, while spending his honeymoon here.

In 1972, faced with a dying timber economy, residents decided to entice tourists—the short main street was given a western theme, capitalizing on the town's ties to *The Virginian* and mining. An architect was hired to preserve the spirit of the valley.

Now the town features false fronts, wooden sidewalks, cattle drives, pack trains, rodeo days, medicine shows, old-time fiddling contests, barn dances, and a Cowboy Jamboree.

Today, children's book author and illustrator Erik Brooks calls Winthrop home.

The Wobblies, members of the Industrial Workers of the World (IWW), fought for workers' rights. Founded by trade unionists, socialists, and anarchists, Wobblies argued for workplace democracy and confrontation. The IWW was the first American labor union that refused to discriminate again foreigners, women, and African Americans.

Wobblies won the 1909 Spokane free-speech fight. They arrived to protest employment agents who preyed on day laborers but were banned from organizing in the streets. More protestors arrived and overloaded the legal system by speaking and getting arrested. Hundreds went to jail; a few died, but the tactic worked: Prisoners were released, and licenses for 19 agents were revoked.

The deadliest battle was the 1916 Everett Massacre. Tired of organizers being arrested and beaten, about 300 Wobblies arrived by steamer from Seattle. They were met on the dock by about 200 temporarily deputized men. A firefight killed 5 to 12 Wobblies and 2 deputies.

In Centralia, American Legionnaires raided the IWW Hall to drive Wobblies out of town on Armistice Day 1919. Six Legionnaires were killed, and the Wobblies were arrested. That night, one Wobblie was turned over to a mob, "tried" at the Elks Club, mutilated, and lynched. His cause of death was listed as suicide.

Until recently, most residents refused to discuss the event in which prominent locals participated. A monument to the Legionnaires was erected in 1924; a mural of lynched Wesley Everest wasn't painted until 1997 over the objections of the American Legion.

Wobblies also were involved in the statewide lumber strike in 1917 over wages and an eight-hour day. The nation's first general strike was in Seattle in 1919. Tens of thousands of workers, mostly in shipyards, walked off their jobs for five days. Police and vigilantes rounded up "the Reds" at the IWW and Socialist Party headquarters, arrested leaders, and closed the labor-owned newspaper.

The Wobblies were never again a force in Washington State, but the phrase "soviet of Washington" refers to the state's liberal tendencies.

Wobblies:

Members of the Industrial Workers of the World fought and died for workers' rights in Washington State.

"Go fly a kite!" resonates well along the Long Beach Peninsula in southwest Washington, which benefits from steady breezes off the Pacific Ocean.

Several towns claim to be the Kite Capital of the World, but only Long Beach has the World Kite Museum and Hall of Fame, the only kite museum in North America.

The 2,500-year-history of kites is captured in words, photographs, and about 1,500 kites, including 700 Japanese, Chinese, and Malaysian varieties. The Japanese kites constitute the most complete collection of their type outside Japan.

The Chinese once used kites to ward off evil spirits and to carry messages to the gods. The Taliban banned them when it controlled Afghanistan. During the U.S. Civil War, the Union Army used them to drop leaflets behind the front lines, urging the Confederates to surrender.

And Orville and Wilbur Wright flew a biplane glider kite as they studied the possibilities of flight.

People have fished with kites, fought with kites, and used them to photograph the inside of volcanoes.

The museum sponsors kite-making workshops, kite-flying events, and demonstrations by experts. Twenty-five kite inventors

and makers are honored in the Hall of Fame. Charlie Brown gets special recognition for his 50 years of kite-flying. Remember the kite-eating tree and the kite that, once Charlie finally got it in the air, spontaneously combusted?

Most kites are flown strictly for fun, but since two humans could create a competition by comparing warts, it was easy to conjure up a kite contest. Long Beach hosts the seven-day Washington State International Kite Festival, which draws the world's best kiters, as well as the Northwest Stunt Kite Championships.

It's fascinating to walk the beach during these competitions and admire the colors, sizes, and shapes of hundreds of kites as well as the inventiveness of the competitors.

World Kite Museum:

The only kite museum in North America is in Long Beach.

It may be the most expensive business park in history.

In the 1970s the Washington Public Power Supply System (WPPSS, pronounced "whoops") set out to build the largest nuclear power plant in U.S. history—three reactors at the Hanford Nuclear Reservation in eastern Washington and two at Satsop, near Elma, in western Washington.

The 1979 nuclear accident at Three Mile Island in Pennsylvania soured public support. And before taxpayers knew what had picked their pockets, the WPPSS project budget soared to $24 billion in the 1980s, high interest rates made the financial situation worse, and an overestimation of electrical demand combined with an emphasis on conservation became a fatal mix.

The ill-fated project was terminated in 1983, and WPPSS defaulted on billions in bonds with only one plant completed at Hanford. Eventually, WPPSS had to place the nuclear equivalent of a classified ad. Imagine, "For Sale: Hundreds of millions of dollars in nuclear power plant equipment. Never used. 20 years old. Make offer."

One buyer was found but went bankrupt before money changed hands. Since no one at that time was building nuclear power plants, WPPSS went to Plan B, and the land ended up in the hands of the Satsop Redevelopment Project.

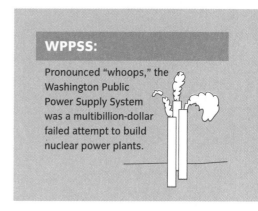

WPPSS:

Pronounced "whoops," the Washington Public Power Supply System was a multibillion-dollar failed attempt to build nuclear power plants.

With 400 acres to develop and 1,200 acres designated as wildlife habitat, Satsop began construction on an environmentally friendly high-tech business park. Already in place were more than one million square feet of building space, wells that could pump up to 14 million gallons a day, and a sewer system for 5,000 workers.

Businesses have begun to trickle into the park. Art projects now brighten some of the gray buildings, and passive recreation projects are in the works.

Today, two mothballed 480-foot cooling towers still dominate the Satsop Valley and can be seen from 100 miles away. At least they have been put to good use. Pilots on international flights from Asia and Australia use the towers to line up their approach to Seattle–Tacoma International Airport.

index